Do you struggle with the leftover pain of childhood wounds? As someone who has worked with men for many years, I can say with confidence that *From Broken Boy to Mended Man* is one of the most powerful resources available to help you understand what happened to you and start healing. Patrick Morley's compassionate approach and practical strategies offer both hope and help to break the cycle for yourself and your family.

DR. TONY EVANS
President of The Urban Alternative and senior pastor of Oak Cliff Bible Fellowship

Pat Morley continues to be one of America's most sane and needed voices on the state of masculinity and manhood. In *From Broken Boy to Mended Man*, he has done it again, tracing our journey from boyhood pain to becoming a whole, healed man.

DAVE RAMSEY
New York Times bestselling author of *The Total Money Makeover*

This is not an endorsement. It is a plea. This book is for you. You must read it. Patrick Morley is one of the most intentional men I have ever known. He doesn't brush his teeth or order breakfast without a plan. This book has been written with the kind of care you'd expect from a surgeon, a fighter pilot, or a multimillion-selling decorated author with something very important to say. You likely don't know it, but you have been waiting a long, long time for this book, from this man. It has the chance to change everything you've thought about everything, starting with your own life. Again, I'm not suggesting you read it. I'm *urging* you to read it. A couple of pages in, you'll understand, and agree. Thank you, Patrick. I needed this book—I and thousands of other men.

ROBERT WOLGEMUTH
Bestselling author of *Finish Line*

Patrick Morley understands what you're going through because he's been there. With precision and simplicity, Patrick will help you understand what happened to you as a child. He will guide you through a hopeful process to heal from your childhood wounds. And he will show you a road map so you can break the cycle of suffering and brokenness for your own family. The pages are packed with practical examples—my favorite is how the hug of a father and a grown son changed the trajectory of an entire family line! *From Broken Boy to Mended Man* will grab you from the first sentence and not let go to the last. Let it guide you to a new freedom and redeem you out of your brokenness.

LOTTIE K. HILLARD, MS
Professional Christian counselor for Patrick Morley

Jesus told us that we need to become like little children, but he most certainly meant the best version of our childhood self—not the broken boy so many of us have been. Pat Morley shows us how to grow up while staying young at heart. God cannot heal the hurts we do not identify. This book will heal old wounds!

MARK BATTERSON
New York Times bestselling author of *The Circle Maker*

FROM BROKEN BOY TO MENDED MAN

FROM BROKEN BOY TO MENDED MAN

A POSITIVE PLAN TO HEAL YOUR
CHIILDHOOD WOUNDS AND BREAK THE CYCLE

PATRICK MORLEY

TYNDALE
MOMENTUM®

A Tyndale nonfiction imprint

Visit Tyndale online at tyndale.com.

Visit Tyndale Momentum online at tyndalemomentum.com.

Tyndale, Tyndale's quill logo, *Tyndale Momentum*, and the Tyndale Momentum logo are registered trademarks of Tyndale House Ministries. Tyndale Momentum is a nonfiction imprint of Tyndale House Publishers, Carol Stream, Illinois.

From Broken Boy to Mended Man: A Positive Plan to Heal Your Childhood Wounds and Break the Cycle

Designed by Jennifer Phelps

Published in association with the literary agency of Wolgemuth & Associates.

Scripture quotations are taken from the Holy Bible, *New International Version,*® *NIV.*® Copyright © 1973, 1978, 1984, 2011 by Biblica, Inc.® Used by permission. All rights reserved worldwide.

For information about special discounts for bulk purchases, please contact Tyndale House Publishers at csresponse@tyndale.com, or call 1-855-277-9400.

Library of Congress Cataloging-in-Publication Data

A catalog record for this book is available from the Library of Congress.

ISBN 978-1-4964-7986-0

Printed in the United States of America

30 29 28 27 26 25 24
7   6   5   4   3   2   1

BROKEN, *ADJECTIVE*

- not functioning properly; out of working order
- fractured, ruptured, torn, smashed, or splintered
- infringed or violated
- confused or disorganized
- interrupted, disrupted, or disconnected
- weakened in strength, spirit, etc.
- exhausted or weakened as through ill-health or misfortune
- (of a relationship) split apart; not intact
- (of a family) disunited or divided by the prolonged or permanent absence of a parent, usually due to divorce or desertion
- overcome with grief or disappointment

MENDED, *VERB*

- to make (something broken, worn, torn, or otherwise damaged) whole, sound, or usable by repairing
- to remove or correct defects or errors in
- to set right; make better; improve
- to progress toward recovery, as a sick person
- (of broken bones) to grow back together
- to improve, as conditions or affairs
- to repair (something broken or unserviceable)
- to improve or undergo improvement; reform
- to heal or recover[1]

To Lottie Hillard,
the compassionate counselor who helped this broken boy
process my pain so I could mend.

CONTENTS

FOREWORD

THROUGH MY FORTY YEARS of counseling men who have experienced childhood wounds, I have never read a book that I have found more helpful for these men than the book you hold in your hands. It is practical, understandable, and doable, I think because it is written by a man who has walked the road.

The reality is that no one chooses their parents. And we are all greatly influenced by those who raised us. That influence may have been positive or negative. We cannot change our childhood history. If you had loving, caring, supportive parents, life will be much easier. If you had parents who inflicted deep emotional wounds, life will be much more difficult. Unfortunately, many men who have childhood wounds will live to repeat the negative example of their parents.

However, the good news is that while you and I are greatly influenced by our parents, our adult life is not determined by our parents' behavior. Most of us know men who had wonderful parents, but instead of following their example, they made bad decisions that wrecked their adult lives. Conversely, it is also possible for men who have deep childhood wounds to make wise decisions and lead productive, fruitful lives. Again, we are influenced by our parents, but our success in life is not determined by our parents' behavior. God has made us free to choose our own destiny.

Most men who grew up with childhood wounds will need "outside help" on their journey to healing and health. Patrick Morley offers such help in *From Broken Boy to Mended Man*. If you will read and apply the steps in this book, I predict that you will break the cycle of childhood wounds. You can become the person you have always wanted to become. You can have healthy relationships. If you choose to make the journey, God will walk with you.

Gary Chapman, PhD
Author of The Five Love Languages

PART 1

UNRAVELING YOUR CHILDHOOD WOUNDS

1

THE FRATERNAL ORDER
OF BROKEN BOYS

THERE ARE MILLIONS OF US. We carry around leftover pain from childhood wounds.

As a result of this unprocessed pain, we act out in ways that damage our relationships. We're easily offended. Fragile. We lash out. We withdraw. We're baffled by our behavior. Frankly, we're not even sure what normal behavior looks like.

We all want to silence the voices of the past, but the way forward is shrouded in mystery. We look at our lives and can't help wondering, *Is this as good as it gets?* We're terrified we might repeat the cycle with our own spouses and children, rather than break it.

What we really want—have always wanted—is for our parents to love us, believe in us, and be proud of us. We ache to be

3

encouraged, respected, and valued. We yearn for their approval and affirmation—to be the gleam in their eyes. That's what you and I need to thrive.

When a young man doesn't get these things from his mom and dad, he ends up as a little boy with a hole. I know. That's what happened to me.

IT'S PERSONAL

When my mother died from cancer, I didn't feel anything. I wasn't sad. I didn't cry. There was no emotional response. Nothing. At the time, I was fifty-three years old.

Knowing something was off, I made an appointment with a counselor to figure out why. Over eight sessions, my counselor helped me process the father and mother wounds I had never been able to put into words. That allowed me to grieve the childhood I had missed. It empowered me to forgive, heal, and make beautiful, lasting changes.

Not understanding our emotions is more common for us men than you might think. Researchers believe that many men are so emotionally impaired that not only do we struggle to express our feelings but we're emotionally blind to what those feelings even are.[1]

Perhaps you also carry around the lingering, hard-to-put-into-words pain of childhood wounds. Maybe your father or mother was not in the picture. Or maybe one or both were neglectful and distant, or angry and abusive, or self-absorbed. Maybe they just didn't know any better. But the result is the same, and you've never gotten over it.

If that's you, I want you to know you're in good company.

Most of the men with whom you will cross paths today had fathers or mothers who failed them. In fact, renowned addiction expert Terence Gorski wrote, "In the United States today . . . it is estimated that approximately 70 to 80 percent come from dysfunctional families."[2]

As many as eight out of every ten men you cross paths with today in your neighborhood, workplace, gym, or church also grew up in dysfunctional homes. You are not alone. Together, we are the fraternal order of broken boys.

What is your starting point today? Is it passivity, resignation, addiction, rage, a critical spirit, poor self-esteem, denial, or lack of confidence? Are you oversensitive to criticism, lashing out when it comes? Do you get moody and withdraw? Are you driven to win acceptance in the world because you didn't get it at home? Are you an overachiever, a protector of the weak, or a champion of lost causes?

Whatever your starting point, the process is the same. The Bible prescribes a process for healing (and preventing) childhood wounds that has been in constant, successful use for thousands of years. Psychologists, psychiatrists, and counselors refine or restate the process, but it's also true that there's really nothing new under the sun. And this process works regardless of your beliefs about God.

HERE'S THE PLAN

In *From Broken Boy to Mended Man*, I'm offering to guide you—as someone who has walked the path already—through this time-tested process. You can take control of your life. You can find healing—starting now. Your wounds may *describe* you, but they don't have to *define* you.

By the end of this journey, you will

- unravel what happened to you,
- understand how you've been wounded,
- see how those wounds affect you and the people you love, and
- develop a positive plan to heal your childhood wounds and break free from any destructive cycles holding you back.

We will also work on building a more compassionate view of our parents, and we'll see how to apply the lessons in a way that empowers us to be better parents to our own children.

Why *compassion*? For longer than I should have, I judged my parents without mercy. But with each passing decade of walking the same roads they had to walk, I've realized that everything is harder than it looks.

Starting in chapter 2, each chapter concludes with discussion and reflection questions to help you process and apply what you're learning. To squeeze the most out of this book, I encourage you to form a small group of men or couples to discuss these questions together. A small group will give you a chance to hear and be heard, to understand and be understood. Over several decades of working with men, I've seen that most meaningful change takes place in small groups. (The "Guide: How to Lead a Discussion Group" in the back of the book has everything you need to get started.) Who are the people with whom you would most like to share your thoughts and feelings as you read this book?

Today, I'm not angry. I'm not bringing to you the rantings of an angry teenager who became an angry man who never meaningfully processed his pain. By going through the process described in this book, I learned how to overcome my anger. You can too.

When we remain stuck in anger at our parents, it's only another small step to start blaming them for all our faults and shortcomings. But more importantly, anger diverts attention from the real issues that need healing. I knew healing is what I ultimately needed—and that's what you need too.

With that in mind, let me tell you why I, too, am part of this fraternal order of broken boys.

MY STORY: THE CLIFFSNOTES

For six years I struggled over whether to write this book. On the one hand, men like me who have grown up in broken or dysfunctional families need help. I've received that help, it has made all the difference, and because helping men is my vocation, I feel compelled to pass it on.

On the other hand, I didn't want to throw my parents under the bus. I loved my parents, and I honestly believe they loved my three younger brothers and me. All parents make mistakes, but I believe they made their mistakes out of ignorance, not malice. They were never trained or discipled in how to parent, nor was it modeled for them. If anything, that's why I want to honor them for doing the best they could.

That said, the damage done to me was the same as if their

actions, or lack of them, had been intentional: I grew up as a practical orphan. Our home was dysfunctional.

As a boy I always felt like I was on my own. I have no recollection of anyone telling me they believed in me, loved me, or were proud of me. I don't even remember being hugged.

I don't recall anyone telling me that my life had meaning, that I was created for a purpose, or that I could do something to make a difference in the world. I don't remember anyone talking to me about knowing God, going to college, or choosing a career.

I'm not so naive as to say with certainty that none of these things ever happened, but I have no recollection of them. However, even if they *did* happen, the fact that I can't remember them is significant in itself.

Eventually, all four of us boys went off the rails. I quit high school in the middle of my senior year and joined the Army. My next brother, Robert, followed in my footsteps. He later died of a heroin overdose. My other two brothers have had more than their fair share of struggles.

Once I left home, I washed my hands of my parents and didn't look back. If not for the influence of my wife, I probably wouldn't have had any contact with my parents at all. The best word to describe our relationship was *estranged*. That whole picture started to change in my early thirties—the beginning of a journey that has led me to share my story with you.

The risk in telling *any* story is that we tend to make ourselves the hero (or victim) and the other party the villain. This is especially true when we start talking about our fathers and mothers.

The tendency, of course, is to give ourselves the benefit of the doubt while holding our parents to a higher standard. But I pledge to give my parents the same respect and benefit of the doubt that I would want from them if they were writing about me. I'm guided by Scriptures that say, "Do everything in love" (1 Corinthians 16:14) and "Honor your father and your mother" (Exodus 20:12). I want to write about my parents with the same grace and respect I hope my children would give me.

Although my mom and dad are no longer living, I think they would strongly approve of this account. I've pictured the three of us in a room, going back and forth over the manuscript, until we could each say, "Yes, that's it—that's the way it really happened. And that's a story that can help others benefit from our mistakes."

That's my goal—to share lessons I learned the hard way so you don't have to. I'm writing to you *not* as a clinician but as an older brother in the fraternal order of broken boys.

Whatever these pages stir inside you, I hope you, too, will share openly with someone else, whether it's your spouse or partner, best friend, small group, or, depending how deep the wounds are, a counselor. That's because most meaningful change takes place in the context of relationships.

Now let me tell you about my counseling sessions. What an eye-opener!

2

A LITTLE BOY WITH A HOLE: NOTES FROM COUNSELING

WHEN MY COUNSELOR ASKED HOW SHE COULD HELP, I responded, "It's pretty simple. My mother died a few months ago. I haven't had any emotional response, and I'd like to know why."

I invested twenty minutes defending my parents' honor, noting that no parents are perfect. Then my counselor started to probe below the surface. For the first time ever, I authentically opened up about my childhood to someone other than my wife.

I confessed that I couldn't remember my parents ever asking questions to find out what was churning inside of me. Nothing about hopes, dreams, or desires. Nothing about what I wanted to do with my life. I'm not saying that never happened, only that I couldn't (and still can't) remember. We were a nonverbal family.

Without guidance, I became an increasingly out-of-control teenager. I ran away from home after the tenth grade, took a job, and rented a room. Every day for dinner, I ate a grilled cheese sandwich at the bowling alley across the street. I had no plan, and I didn't care.

The runaway experience lasted two weeks before my dad found me and said he and my mother wanted me to come home. I couldn't believe it! I honestly thought that bridge was burned. That's how naive I was. It was such a wonderful feeling that they wanted me back—as fresh today as the moment my dad said it.

But I continued to spiral. A year later, Orange County deputies delivered me home, unable-to-stand-up drunk. That incident was just the tip of the iceberg.

High school was a constant tug-of-war between wanting to find a purpose and the all-consuming feeling, *What's the point?* I skipped all or part of seventy-three days in my junior year and then quit school altogether in the middle of my senior year.

My main memory of childhood is feeling I was on my own to figure things out. I didn't have a clue. On the other hand, I didn't know any better—I was just a kid.

At this point, I expected my counselor to jump in and tell me how to fix it. Instead, she continued to ask questions. Because she guided me and gave me time to unravel my thoughts, I started to feel like I could trust her. So I kept talking.

WHAT'S REALLY GOING ON

Eventually, I was able to articulate that my biggest struggle was not being able to recall feeling deeply loved as a child.

In fact, I have no recollection of hearing the words "I love you" until I was thirty-five years old. (I'll explain the beautiful way that came about at the beginning of chapter 6.)

My second biggest struggle was not feeling like my parents were proud of me. The first time I heard the words "I'm proud of you," I was forty-seven years old. (I'll explain how that happened and the wonderful change that brought about in chapter 12.)

Frankly, as a kid, I had no reason to know parents are supposed to speak words of love and affirmation, so it's not like I expected them. I didn't know what I was missing, because I had nothing to compare it to.

With the lack of verbal love and affirmation out in the open to my counselor, I shared that we were not a physically affectionate family either. For example, I can't remember ever being hugged. Again, not remembering doesn't mean it didn't happen, but I learned it's significant that there's no childhood memory of my parents comforting me with a hug.

THOUGHTS A LITTLE BOY CAN'T HANDLE

A signature memory of my childhood took place when I was about ten. I was putting on my uniform for a Little League baseball game. My parents said they wanted to watch me play. (Apparently, they didn't regularly attend my games.) I told them I didn't want them at my game and pleaded with them not to come until I was in tears. Finally, they gave in and said they wouldn't come.

Then I threaded my baseball glove onto my handlebars and cried for the entire eight-minute bike ride to the Little League field because they weren't coming.

My counselor asked, "What do you think this means?"

"I have no idea. I was hoping you could tell me!"

Then she told me this story:

A pastor had a son named Noah. He told his son he would take him fishing. The little boy was so excited, he woke the next morning at 5:30, bounding around the house, getting ready.

About 6:30 the phone rang. His father, the pastor, answered the phone and said, "Yes, I understand. Yes, yes, okay. I'll be right there." And then he hung up and left on an emergency appointment.

That night at dinner, the little boy—who had been bounding around the house that morning—was now bent over his food, moping and looking sad. His mother said to his father, "Do you realize you forgot to take Noah fishing this morning?"

The pastor was mortified. He said, "I cannot believe I forgot that, Noah. I am so sorry. I'll make it up to you. We'll go fishing another day."

The little boy said, "Oh, that's okay. I don't like fishing anyway."

My counselor asked, "What do you think is going on there?"

"Again, I have no idea. You're the paid professional! You tell me!"

She said, "No, I want you to think about it."

I honestly could not figure it out.

She explained that—and this is the crux of the matter—a

little boy cannot handle the thought, cannot accept the thought, cannot live with the idea that his father doesn't really care enough about him to want to be with him. So instead, he substitutes the idea that he doesn't like fishing.

"In other words," she said, "he can't just say, 'My dad doesn't want to be with me.' A little boy can't take that. So instead, he says, 'I don't like fishing.'"

Then my counselor asked, "What do you think was going on when you told your parents not to come to the ball field?"

"I think I'm starting to get the picture," I responded.

My counselor thought that at a very early age I decided I wasn't that important to my mom and dad. She said, "A little boy can't handle the thought, *My mother and father don't delight in me; I am not loved*." So instead, I substituted, *I really don't want them at my game*.

I had decided, *If they don't need me, then I don't need them either*.

And from the moment of that decision, I started distancing myself from my parents. As my counselor explained, I was protecting myself from the pain of thinking I wasn't important to my parents. They didn't spend much time with me, so I wouldn't spend much time with them.

Did I want them to watch my game and shamelessly cheer for me? Of course I did. Desperately. But when the proverb says, "Folly is bound up in the heart of a child" (Proverbs 22:15), it's no joke.

And without proper training, parents can make foolish mistakes too.

STRUGGLING WITH DENIAL

My counselor used the word "failure" to describe the parenting I experienced, even if it wasn't intentional. "Your parents didn't love you enough," she said. "They might have been good *people*, but they weren't good enough *parents*."

"But what about when Dad pursued me when I ran away?" I pushed back.

"Did he really want you back," she asked, "or did he only want to restore order in his own life?"

Similarly, she concluded I was not mothered by my mom. The lack of verbal affection, touch, and time indicated a kind of betrayal—even if it wasn't deliberate.

I protested sharply and told her that when I was voted king of my sixth-grade class, my mom made a special cape for me by hand. She dyed a bedsheet red and then sewed gold-colored fringe around the edge.

My counselor responded, "It could be that she wanted to be *known* as a good mother."

As I shared more, she pointed out that emotional neglect is a form of abandonment. She saw gross abandonment in my life. She said, directly, "Pat, you've been hurt, maybe abused."

I was floored.

Is that too harsh? I wondered. *Could it be true? Am I just denying it? Am I confused because my parents genuinely were nice people?*

I figured I must not have presented things in the right light. I felt the need to protect my parents' reputation. So I shared that when my mother's health was failing, I went to great lengths to call her every day and to visit her every weekend. We had great talks.

My counselor pushed back, "That doesn't necessarily mean she loved you. It might just mean she loved you loving her." She then made a distinction between loving and enjoying being loved.

I thought, *Is she trying to provoke me to rethink my story? Maybe I don't miss my mom because I was the pursuer, not the pursued.* But that thought only made me feel even more uncomfortable and disrespectful.

She pressed on, "Your parents betrayed you twice—first by not investing in you, and then by wanting a return that exceeded their investment. I think you are in deep denial of this betrayal."

Then she said something that reverberated in my mind: "Something is missing when you don't feel precious and deeply cared for. *You are a little boy with a hole.*"

She explained that a physically or emotionally abandoned child will become either self-sufficient or stymied in life because they feel something is wrong with them. "You clearly ended up on the self-sufficient path," she told me. "You are not the product of good parenting but a miracle."

She continued, "You're able to love others and empathize so well because you have suffered greatly. Often helping *others* grieve helps someone like *you* grieve, who has not fully faced their pain."

The emotions that hadn't surfaced when my mom died were buried somewhere, she assured me. She wanted me to allow those feelings to surface—not to manufacture them, but not to control or stifle them either.

Counseling had challenged all my long-held perceptions about my childhood. I walked out with a lot to process.

THE BEGINNING OF GRIEF

Over the next few days, I pored over and prayerfully reflected on the notes I had taken.

In a matter of hours, my counselor had demolished the story I had constructed to shield myself from not feeling precious. I was finally able to accept that my parents had failed me. We were a dysfunctional family, but none of us knew it at the time.

That released a cacophony of very confused thoughts and feelings. Here are the impressions I scribbled down in a journal at that time:

- My parents didn't discourage me, but that doesn't mean they encouraged me.
- I don't remember being comforted.
- I don't remember being held, told I was loved, or told I made them proud.
- I don't remember their coming to my games and activities or spending time with me. Just because they spent some time with me doesn't mean they spent enough. It's like they made the down payment but defaulted on the balance. It's like they thought they could build a $1,000 boy for only $100. They invested a little, thinking it would return a lot.
- I was betrayed by such nice people.
- I experienced gross abandonment, despite so many good memories of family.
- I suffered greatly because I felt so alone and on my own.
- I rejected them because I felt they didn't want (or need) me.

- I pushed them away. I always thought this was at my initiation, but I pushed them away because I couldn't handle the thought that they really didn't want me. As a small boy, I wanted to be wanted so badly. I wanted them at my games. As a teen, I wanted them to rescue me from my downward slide. Why didn't they rescue me? (Tears came as I wrote this.)
- I have thought that because I was a priority at some level, my teenage meltdown was all my fault—*I* was the one who messed up. I've always blamed myself. But they were the parents; I was the child. They should have been the ones who made it work. It wasn't up to me, though I thought it was. (I was still in tears at this point.)

By the time I finished journaling, I wasn't angry—just sad. But finally, I was able to have a good cry. It was the end of denial and the beginning of grief.

THE VOW

I was now ready to accept that I had been neglected. My parents let me down, and that was a betrayal—however unintentional. But I also realized that I'd been held back by this wound for too long. And I had found my raw point. Somewhere along the way, I'd taken a vow: "If you're not going to give me what I need, then I'm done with you."

As I discussed all of this with the counselor at our next session, she said, "You wrote your mother off because she let you down. But you apply that vow to all who remind you of your wound. You need to repent of that vow you made."

It was my "aha" moment. Suddenly it dawned on me why it always felt so raw and painful to be let down or rejected and why I was oversensitive to perceived negative social cues or betrayal. All of it served as a reminder of feeling rejected, unloved, not precious, and not valuable.

It had always felt incredibly risky to accept someone's delight in me. *What if it isn't sincere? What if it is later withdrawn?* As a result, I was regularly edgy and suspicious, even around friends. I was *expecting* people to let me down—almost *waiting* on them to remind me of my wound. And when they did, I was severely tempted to cut them out of my life.

I knew I had a choice to make. Yes, I had a wound. But at some point, we each must decide if we're going to stay frozen in the past. We must decide if we're going to live like perpetual victims or take responsibility for our lives. That's the real point—do we want to be victims or victors?

That day, on the drive back to my office, I prayed,

Lord, I did make this vow regarding my parents: "If you're not going to give me what I need, then I'm done with you." I confess that I have used that vow as a sword and as a coat of armor. By faith, I choose to change my mind. I do repent. Please cleanse me of all the harm done to me and by me from that vow. For the glory of Jesus, amen.

My prayer was sincere, and the relief was instant.

Still, some wounds are so deep they're like a game of whack-a-mole—they keep popping up even when we think we're done with them. For example, while I rarely act on it, I'm still tempted to cut people out of my life if they give me the wrong vibe.

That's why repentance is not a one-and-done concept. You may find yourself re-grieving certain wounds—sometimes as though you've never grieved at all but other times as an echo of the previous pain. This can be especially true if your parents are living and haven't changed.

Yes, there *is* healing, though many of us will still walk with a limp. But there can be joy in that limp, as we'll explore later.

In the chapters ahead, we'll unravel what happened to you and why, then how you can heal and break the cycle. But first, consider the reflection and discussion questions on the next page.

REFLECTION AND DISCUSSION

1. Describe what it was like to grow up in your home.

2. If you have children, what's it like for them to be growing up in your home? Are you repeating or breaking the cycle of your own childhood? If you've been on the wrong track, don't despair. In the pages ahead you'll find a hopeful, practical plan to put you on the right track.

3

HOW OUR PARENTS WOUNDED US

MOST OF THE BOYS in our neighborhood, like me, were in fifth grade. But a few, like Nunny, were older. Nunny was small but fierce, a neighborhood bully who terrified us all.

One day Nunny announced he was going to beat me up and started swinging. I tried to escape by running into our house, but my dad forced me back outside to fight. It was Dad's way of teaching me to stand up for myself.

Several neighbors sat on lawn chairs and spectated as Nunny and I locked in a titanic battle that spread across several front yards.

What started as a fistfight quickly turned into a wrestling match as we both began to tire. I couldn't beat him up, but because of my fear-induced adrenaline, he couldn't beat me up either. Eventually we were both too exhausted to continue and, without fanfare, we stopped. Although Nunny became increasingly violent as a teen—for example, cutting another boy with a broken whiskey bottle—he never bothered me again.

I'll never forget that. I went home to find protection, but my dad made me fight. It worked out, but never in a million years can I picture doing that to our son, John. My counselor was right. Something was dysfunctional—even if not intended.

THE PROBLEM

We all know folly is bound up in the heart of a child. Parents are responsible to correct that folly but without crushing their child's soul.

Unfortunately, many parents were never properly parented themselves. They have no model for how to create a safe, healthy home. They inherited intergenerational brokenness from their parents. Then they couldn't break the cycle and passed on some (or all) of that brokenness to their children—you and me. And that puts us at risk of repeating the vicious cycle all over again.

Who knows how many generations ago our families began these cycles of dysfunction? Regardless, what really matters is *Now what?* You can put a stop to your family's intergenerational dysfunction, but first you must become an emotionally, mentally, and spiritually healthy person yourself. That includes dealing with your own childhood wounds so you don't repeat the cycle and pass on those wounds to your own children.

What matters right now is that you can do this—you can break the curse. You can receive help. You can become a healthy man. The first step? You'll need to get your head around what went wrong. Because if you're trying to solve the wrong problem, you can only succeed by accident.

If you had chest pains, the doctors would never treat you without a proper diagnosis. Diagnosis precedes treatment. That's why in this chapter I'm going to help you diagnose the *cause* of your childhood wounds—what should have happened, why it didn't, and how you see your parents as a result. Then in the following two chapters, we're going to explore the *effect* those wounds have had on you personally.

WHAT YOU NEEDED AS A CHILD

Parenting is a sacred promise to prioritize a child's physical, mental, emotional, social, financial, moral, and spiritual health. Your parents* had a duty to provide for and protect you. They had a responsibility to help you grow strong and healthy in mind, body, and spirit. They also had the privilege of giving you a sense of well-being and an opportunity to create a family environment where you could thrive.

To thrive, children need *love*, *structure*, *roots*, and *wings*. Most of us have heard the question "Is it nature or nurture?" Love, structure, roots, and wings are the building blocks of nurture.

Parental love produces a feeling that you are precious, structure helps you know where your guardrails are, roots offer stability to flourish, and wings prepare you to be a man.

---

* Since there are too many types of households—such as single parents, guardians, and foster parents—to name each time we talk about the people who raised you, we will use the plural form of parents to streamline. I ask you to please adjust for your own growing-up experience.

Love

Every time a TV show ends with two people making up and hugging each other, I tear up. Love is the umbrella over everything. No force in the world is more powerful than a healthy, loving relationship.

The love that fills a healthy home is overt and unconditional. If you grew up in a love-filled home, you felt precious, valuable, and believed in, like you were the gleam in your parents' eyes.

You regularly heard verbal affection. "I love you," "I believe in you," and "I'm proud of you" reverberated off the walls of your home. Your parents consistently affirmed you with words of encouragement, affection, respect, value, validation, and approval.

You also regularly received physical affection. You were hugged. Your mother kissed your skinned knee and assured you everything was going to be okay. Your father gave you high fives and wrestled with you on the family-room floor.

As my counselor said, "Mothers give their sons grounding and a sense of well-being; fathers give them confidence."

Your parents spent time with you. They went to your school activities, played games, and took you fun places.

They mentored and coached you around the dinner table. And there were laughs—lots and lots of laughs.

Of course, every healthy family also has disagreements, conflict, behavior issues, and differences of opinion. That's normal.

But you thrived because your parents' love made you feel safe in the deepest parts of your mind, soul, and spirit. You felt affirmed.

REFLECTION EXERCISE:

In general, did you feel like your parents loved you as a child?

| never | rarely | sometimes | usually | always |

Go ahead and select an answer even if you're not 100 percent sure.

Structure

When our children were still in diapers, I heard Christian counselor and author Larry Crabb comment on the proverb that says, "Folly is bound up in the heart of a child." He said, "Children need to know, 'Yes, I love you, and no, you can't have your own way.'"

A healthy home is filled with clear-cut structure. If you grew up in a well-structured home, your parents were predictable. You always knew where you stood, what the rules were, what was out of bounds, and what to expect if you disobeyed.

But you never felt like discipline was rejection. If anything, your parents went overboard to make sure you understood why you were being disciplined. They helped you understand what was going on inside your heart that caused you to misbehave.

Sure, every parent makes mistakes. Sometimes they are too structured, and sometimes not enough.

But you thrived because you always knew what to expect, and you knew your parents would try to be fair and even-handed. That structure gave you confidence.

REFLECTION EXERCISE:

In general, did you feel like your parents provided you with good structure?

never	rarely	sometimes	usually	always

If not, was it too much or not enough?

Roots

My wife and I planted seven live oak trees in our yard. That's because we live in a hurricane corridor, and we wanted trees that would grow deep roots so they wouldn't get knocked down.

A healthy home has roots. Roots build character, perseverance, determination, diligence, and resilience. If you grew up in a home with deep roots, no matter how much you got knocked down at school, you always felt like things would be okay once you got home. Your parents made you feel secure, safe, and stable. They protected you from worldly ways and from people who might otherwise prey on you.

Your parents made sure you always had food, shelter, and clothing—even if they had to go without. They made sure you received a good education. They gave you moral, relational, vocational, financial, and spiritual foundations. You felt anchored.

You thrived because your parents *nurtured* you to maturity. They did all this while considering your *nature*—the unique temperament, personality, and aptitudes with which you came into the world.

In general, do you feel like your parents gave you roots?

never	rarely	sometimes	usually	always

Wings

My wife and I were excited when we dropped our daughter off at a small university known as much for building character as for educating. The director of counseling met separately with the parents of first-year students. She rattled off seven developmental tasks they would focus on:

- Growing competence
- Managing emotions
- Developing autonomy
- Establishing identity
- Fostering interpersonal relationships
- Discovering a sense of purpose
- Cultivating personal integrity

But in a healthy home, your parents had already been working on these developmental tasks for years. Your parents made you feel ready to take on the world.

A healthy home gives children wings. Your parents helped you experiment until you found a few things you love and do well—whether in academics, sports, or the arts. They also helped you develop social skills, such as looking people in the eyes when you're speaking or being spoken to. They nurtured your emotional intelligence and situational awareness.

They talked to you about the meaning of life. Purpose. God. Love. Sexuality. Right and wrong. They listened to you—*really* listened—and you felt heard and understood. That put wind in your sails, even when you didn't get your own way.

If you grew up in a home that gave you wings, you entered adulthood with confidence, excitement, and anticipation. When you flew out of the nest, you were guided by the philosophies, values, and beliefs your parents instilled in you.

Obviously, these tasks are never complete, but when you left home, you felt prepared to thrive as a man because you knew who you were and what you needed to do. You were ready to be independent. And coupled with the love, structure, and roots you received from your parents, you have a lot below the waterline—courage, inner strength, and self-confidence.

REFLECTION EXERCISE:
Did your parents give you wings?

never	rarely	sometimes	usually	always

We've just explored what *should* have happened. A man who rated himself highly in love, structure, roots, and wings would say, "My parents were affirming" or "My parents were encouraging." That's positive parenting.

But what if you can't say that? You are part of the fraternal order of broken boys because your parents made mistakes (or failed altogether) in one, some, or all of these four areas.

The end goal, of course, is to heal. But first, let me help you understand what went wrong.

HOW PARENTS CREATE WOUNDS

Here are seven generalized descriptions of negative parenting. They will overlap, so don't be surprised if you identify the way you were raised with more than one profile. Not every description will apply, but as you read, ask yourself, *Was this generally the case?* I suggest you read with a pen or highlighter and mark the statements that make you think, *Yep, that's me.*

"My Parents Were Passive"

Your parents were under-involved. They simply were not there for you. They were in the home physically, but they were distant and emotionally unavailable. They were not engaged with you. You didn't regularly hear words of love, affection, and affirmation. You felt like you were on your own and had to fend for yourself, and you assumed this was your fault.

Your childhood was not filled with happy memories of all the things you did together as a family. No one tossed a ball with you in the backyard. No one attended your school activities. You were left on your own to roam.

Perhaps your parents were nice, or perhaps they were mean or abusive. In any case, they were passive. They didn't care enough. You didn't get the support you needed. You were neglected.

"My Parents Were Absent"

Your parents were not in the picture. Whether by divorce, death, mental illness, or choice, they were physically or emotionally absent.

Your parents were so absorbed in their own lives that they didn't have time for you. You came home to an empty house, made your own meals, and had to take responsibility to do your own homework and get to and from school.

You were not the apple of their eye. You were not the center of their universe. They were busy. Your mom or dad (or both) pursued money, career, position, prestige, and worldly accolades. They sacrificed you on the altar of their success. Or they gave in to other addictions. Success addicts and drug addicts often display similar obsessions.[1] Workaholic or alcoholic—there's not much difference.

A man told me a sad story. His best friend died tragically while they were attending college together. At the funeral, his friend's father, who was a titan in the business world, approached him and asked, "Weren't you and my son best friends?"

He said, "Yes, sir."

Then the father said, "I was so busy building my business that I never really got to know him. Could you please tell me a little about my son?"

"My Parents Were Permissive"

Your parents let you get away with almost anything short of murder. This is "Yes, I love you, and yes, you can have your own way" parenting. Or maybe for you love wasn't part of the equation—just "You can have your own way."

In either case, you suffered from a lack of structure. You didn't know the boundaries. You grew up without guardrails. When I was dating my wife, she said, "I think your parents gave you too much say." And she was right.

When my friend Chace was eight years old, his parents gave him unrestricted Internet access. When he turned eleven, he and his friends started looking at pornography. The only things

Chace learned about how to treat girls came from watching YouTube and R-rated movies.

When he turned fourteen, his mother slipped a pamphlet about sex across the car seat without making eye contact. She only said, "You should read this." That was the full extent of his sex education—not a word from his dad. When he was sixteen, Chace had sex for the first time with a younger girl from his school in her parents' bedroom. She came home to an empty house every day, just like he did.

"My Parents Were Enabling"

Your parents smothered you with attention because (to them) you could do no wrong. They showered you with freedom, things, and the faulty impression that you were the center of the universe. But they didn't provide enough structure to teach you how to fend for yourself and take personal responsibility.

Your parents gave too much *and* required too little. You never faced accountability because they always rescued you. If permissive parents *let* you have your own way, enabling parents *helped* you have your own way.

In a healthy home, parents help their children do things they *can't* do for themselves, but they require them to do what they *can* and *should* do for themselves. They also require them to take responsibility when they do something they should *not* have done.

In your home, your parents perpetually let things slide. They enabled you to not do what you could and should have done for yourself, such as make your bed, do chores, and not talk sassy.

They also enabled you by not requiring you to take responsibility for things you shouldn't have done. This was the issue for two teenage brothers who threw rocks and shattered the outside security lights on my neighbor's house. When they got caught, their dad made excuses for them, so they got away with it.

"My Parents Were Angry"

Your parents were usually upset about something—or their anger was always lurking just below the surface, ready to erupt. Anger is a normal human emotion. Jesus experienced anger. But one or both of your parents didn't process their anger well. Even if they encouraged you with verbal and physical affection, their anger stole it back.

They could be peevish, petty, and prickly. They easily and regularly lost their temper, but you never knew what triggered them. They were serial overreactors. This made you cower.

They were routinely harsh. I saw a mother at a grocery store, screaming at her small child who had accidentally bumped into some cans that fell to the floor. Your parents were like that on a regular basis, exploding over even small infractions.

Family strife, conflict, or even violence were everyday occurrences. Sometimes you felt like a tethered goat—you couldn't escape and were just waiting for the next verbal tirade.

You were spanked or hit in anger. Discipline was unpredictable and arbitrary. Your parents turned your childhood into chaos and conflict. Perhaps addictions were involved. Because you always felt like you had to walk on eggshells, you preferred playing at your friends' houses and not your own.

"My Parents Were Demanding"

Your parents were overbearing, demanding, and controlling. Their list of rules gave new meaning to the term "strict." They didn't have *conversations* with you; they issued *commands*. You were told to obey and not ask questions. You were not encouraged to think or speak for yourself.

If permissive parents are too lax, demanding parents are legalistic. You felt unusually high demands for conformity and outward obedience. They were authoritarian and didn't have use for excuses.

You learned not to ask too many questions, have a different opinion, or speak unless spoken to. You were not allowed to just be a kid—to be yourself.

Your parents were pushy. Domineering. Manipulative. You felt like you had to perform to make your parents happy and win their approval, but your best was never good enough. You knew what was expected, but you had no support. You feared failing but didn't get affirmation when you did well. In fact, your parents often made you feel like you should have done better.

They frequently withheld love and even used it as a weapon to manipulate you. As a friend told me, "No matter what I did, I could never make my dad happy."

"My Parents Were Belittling"

While emotional neglect is passive, your parents actively invalidated your emotions with criticism. They teased you, mocked you, and regularly made jokes at your expense. You felt like you were a disappointment—like they were sorry you were born.

You didn't know how to make them happy. When you did something that made them unhappy, they would exhale exaggerated sighs to show their disapproval or even disgust. Everything you did was questioned or called into doubt, and you never felt like you had done enough. Regular critiques destroyed your self-esteem. Verbal affection was sparse.

When you did try to do something positive, they put you down. Your mother told you, "You will never amount to anything. You're just like your father."

Your parents tortured you with their caustic put-downs. You were regularly shamed for your mind, for the way you looked, or for some other characteristic over which you had no control. Sometimes they did this publicly.

Your parents took out frustrations about how their own lives were turning out by ridiculing you. You were their scapegoat.

They played favorites and encouraged sibling rivalry. As a result, your siblings may have experienced your parents differently. When I was first getting to know my best friend, Jim, he asked one day, "Which of your children do you love the most?" I was dumbfounded. Such an idea was foreign to me, but he asked because his parents had picked his siblings over him. That was his experience.

Playing favorites can happen in any of these negative parenting profiles. For example, you may have a brother or sister who describes your parents as enabling because they were a favorite, while you experienced your parents as belittling. Unequal treatment creates envy, jealousy, rivalries, and sometimes even hatred that can last for decades.

CONCLUSION

Now you have a foundation to compare how your parents raised you to how you should have been raised. Sobering, isn't it?

Answer the following questions, and then we will unpack how these parenting mistakes are affecting you today.

REFLECTION AND DISCUSSION

1. How would you describe your relationship with your father, mother, or caregiver today? For example: cordial, strained, warm, estranged.

2. What was your childhood missing in the areas of love, structure, roots, or wings?

3. Which of the seven generalized descriptions of negative parenting are most relevant for you (e.g., "my parents were passive"), and why?

4

UNDERSTANDING YOUR WOUNDS—PART 1

OUR SON PLAYED POINT GUARD on his high school basket-ball team. One day my mother and father came to watch a game. They had never seen our son play basketball. My parents sat between my wife and me in the bleachers—my wife was next to Dad, and I was next to Mom.

During the game, I was telling my mother how proud we were of John for practicing so diligently, for working on his leadership skills, for being so industrious, and for becoming a team player. I concluded, "We let him know every day how much we love him and how proud we are of him."

After a few moments of silence, my mom said to nobody in particular, "You know, when our four boys were growing up, I don't think we told them often enough that we were proud of them."

A bomb exploded inside my head. I wanted to scream, "Mom, I'm sitting right here! I was one of those four boys! Why are you talking about me in the third person?"

Then I thought, *Why didn't you do that? It would have been so easy! Just to let us know that you loved us and were proud of us! Why didn't you do that?*

Then it occurred to me: *It's not too late, Mom! You can do it now. You can tell me now!*

But instead of saying any of that, I said nothing.

NAMING YOUR WOUNDS

How do childhood wounds affect us as adults? Some of us are angry. Some are sad. Many of us are both—and confused. If your parents were self-absorbed, angry, or abusive, that might make your emotions easier to understand. Or maybe, like me, you're confused and feel guilty for being so upset because your parents really were nice people. Like me at that basketball game, you say nothing.

Understanding how you've been wounded is key to healing. We don't want to wallow in our wounds, but neither do we want to try to macho our way around them.

There's no universally accepted list of how childhood wounds may have affected you. Scholarly literature offers many helpful models, systems, theories, and schools of thought. But you can also quickly find yourself overwhelmed and confused.

For our purposes, we're going to look at nine major

characteristics of men with childhood wounds. Of course, it's important to add a caveat that there may also be other reasons you have these characteristics. Not everything that's wrong with us is our parents' fault (more on this in chapter 11).

That said, the following characteristics are especially present in men whose parents failed to meet their needs for love, structure, roots, and wings:

1. You have a hard time believing people really care about you.
2. You are oversensitive and often misread what people intend.
3. You are easily angered.
4. You're not sure what healthy male behavior looks like.
5. You're insecure and need constant reassurance.
6. You have dramatic mood swings and don't know why.
7. You're either "the responsible son" or especially immature for your age.
8. You can't get rid of the negative voices in your head.
9. You've cut yourself off from family members emotionally or physically.

These characteristics are not who you are—your identity, personality, and character. Rather, they're what has been done to you. They are *symptoms* left over from growing up in a dysfunctional home. That means that once you identify, diagnose, and name them, you can begin the process of healing.

Some wounds heal quickly. Others take longer. And you will think some wounds are healed, but then they will rear their ugly heads and need to be processed all over again, but each time the wound will shrink. It's a process—one we will fully explore.

So, once again, I suggest you take a pen or highlighter and mark those parts of the following descriptions that resonate with you. They're the unwanted thoughts and behaviors you will work through in the following chapters.

Take your time. Not every characteristic will apply, of course, and I encourage you to add others that come to mind.

1. YOU HAVE A HARD TIME BELIEVING PEOPLE REALLY CARE ABOUT YOU

The first stage of highly regarded psychologist Erik Erikson's theory of human development is "trust vs. mistrust."[1] Early in life, a child decides whether the world is a safe or dangerous place. If people do not care about your needs when you are young and vulnerable, the stage is set for you to look at the world with suspicion, fear, and mistrust.[2]

So if one or both of your parents didn't care (or care enough), it's no surprise you have doubts and suspicions that anyone else would care either. In fact, today you are wary of people who seem to care. You don't trust their motives. You're waiting for the thud of that other shoe to drop.

You find it difficult to trust people's sincerity when they express genuine affection for you. It's risky to accept someone's delight in you: *What if it's fake? What if it's real, but I don't measure up or can't perform to their satisfaction? What if they change their mind? Then what?*

You lack self-confidence in relationships. You're still unsure that you're okay, a good person, worth helping, or worth caring about—even if you're a proven leader with significant skills and accomplishments. You're on high alert, and you struggle to distinguish real affection from fake intimacy.

Because you fear repeating the cycle of pain, like me, you tend to feel reserved or guarded when you walk into a room. Everyone has self-doubts, but yours are exaggerated. You often feel left out, excluded, out of the loop, overlooked, uninvited. You assume, *They don't want me.* Sometimes you continue down that rabbit hole and develop paranoid thoughts.

You have difficulty developing close friendships (although once you do, you are the most fiercely loyal friend someone could have). You keep to yourself. When people don't give you enough positive feedback, you assume they will let you down and abandon you, and you have experiences to back this up.

You're insecure about where you stand with people—even those closest to you. Even your spouse. That's how bad it can get.

To protect yourself from this pain, you've walled yourself in and others out. At times, you feel starved for love and friendship, but the risk of being hurt seems greater than the reward of letting someone in. You made a vow: if people don't need you, then you don't need them.

Some love-starved and approval-deprived children grow up overly dependent and willing to do just about anything to win the affection and approval of others. Others, like me, end up on the self-sufficient path. Both ways are broken. But it doesn't have to stay that way. In the pages ahead, you will learn the steps that can liberate you from this debilitating characteristic.

As you reflect on your own wounds, to what extent do you have a hard time believing people really care about you?

never	rarely	sometimes	usually	always

Again, choose an answer now, even if you aren't completely sure.

2. YOU ARE OVERSENSITIVE AND OFTEN MISREAD WHAT PEOPLE INTEND

David grew up unsure of himself. As an adult, when David would walk into a room with his own four children, he always found himself sitting alone after ten or fifteen minutes. He asked, "What's wrong with me?"

David was oversensitive and, as a result, he couldn't read the room. He would assume the worst, make pouty comments, and overreact when he felt disrespected.

Here's what it's like to be oversensitive: You live with chronic emotional pain. Your perceptions of people's intentions are distorted, and your feelings get hurt easily. You may or may not be good at concealing this hurt.

You regularly assume the worst motives for people's actions. You're guarded and look for any perceived slight, criticism, betrayal, or negative social cue. People's slights remind you of your parents. You've never been taught how to handle criticism correctly and don't respond well.

You take things too personally. When someone turns down

your request or picks someone else, you wonder, *Is something wrong with me? Do they know something that I don't?*

You are not emotionally resilient, so you get down easily. You feel sorry for yourself and are quick to have a pity party. You nurse hurts and hold a grudge. You can be slow to forgive, and you feel bitter about the injustice you've suffered.

You overreact when people question you. People need to choose their words carefully around you. You are prickly, condescending, patronizing, pouty, sarcastic, or all of these. People can tell you are wounded, bruised, and fragile. The more you overreact, the more people shy away from you. Then, you feel your suspicions are confirmed, so you overreact even more. Your acts of self-sabotage spiral into a vicious, self-fulfilling prophecy.

As an adult, many people have let you down, not kept their word, not been there for you when you needed them. Many walked away from friendships without saying a word, as though your relationship meant nothing. Unfortunately, that reinforces the "nobody loves me, nobody cares" narrative.

In reality, often the perceived negative social cues have nothing to do with you personally. For example, the other person might be distracted, struggling with their own crisis, or just too tired to talk. Or a friend might have needed to make a change in his life, but that meant spending less time with you. This felt like a personal rejection, and you felt abandoned. These experiences serve as a reminder that you grew up feeling rejected, unloved, not highly valued, and not precious.

But you also ignore *positive* social cues. You deflect compliments. You have a hard time believing people are sincere when they say nice things about you.

Author and professor James Garbarino wrote in *Lost Boys* that an abused or neglected boy may develop a "code" of four chronic responses to cope with the world around him—two of which we've just illustrated, and the other two we'll illustrate in the next section:

- He becomes hypersensitive to negative social cues.
- He is oblivious to positive social cues.
- He develops a repertory of aggressive behaviors to pull out when threatened.
- He concludes that aggression is a successful way to get what he wants.[3]

Which of these four chronic coping responses do you use? For me, the first three bullets are characteristics I've had to surrender and resurrender to God. I openly admit that I am oversensitive to feeling rejected, even when that's not really what's going on, and I take things personally. My natural tendency is to look for cues that reinforce my predisposition to not trust people.

And to my regret, except for those who have earned my trust over the long haul, I still generally assume that people will let me down. Unless I'm walking in the power of the Holy Spirit, I can struggle to believe positive cues that people really care about me personally.

In the pages ahead we'll explore how you can manage this type of oversensitivity.

To what extent are you oversensitive, often misreading what people intend?

never	rarely	sometimes	usually	always

3. YOU ARE EASILY ANGERED

Drew had too much autonomy when he was a child. Without structure and discipline, his pride grew, and he became a cocky teenager. He walked around with a chip on his shoulder, lashing out whenever he was challenged. His parents did not correct him.

Perhaps you were like Drew and always got your own way (not enough structure), or you experienced the opposite and rarely or never got your own way (too much structure).

As a result, anger is your baseline. You're always close to the boiling point because of repressed, unresolved feelings from previous offenses. Little things set you off, even when you wish you could take them in stride. For example, when a store clerk greets you with indifference or, even worse, disrespect, you feel the bile of anger rising in your throat.

You find it difficult to regulate your emotions, and you tend to be overly aggressive and argumentative, especially when dealing with a person who won't invest time into understanding where you're coming from. Your anger can be explosive, volatile, and way out of proportion to what sets you off.

You've sworn countless times the angry outbursts will not continue, but they do. And each time you lash out, you feel more guilty and ashamed.

That said, you may be able to stuff your anger when it's in your best interest, such as at work. Personally, I've never lost it at work, but I have gone through seasons when I regularly did so at home.

You aren't sure *what* to do but don't like asking for help, because you don't want anyone to think you need it. Burying your feelings allows you to not face the fact that you don't know how to process your anger in a healthy way. This keeps your temper even closer to the boiling point.

Yet you're a strong person. You have pulled yourself up by the bootstraps. You often feel repulsed by people who are weak when they don't have to be and won't make something of themselves. Your antennae are always up for someone else's arrogance and fake intimacy. You have no patience with sappy, oversharing people.

You are highly aggressive in sports or other competitive situations. You engage in risky behavior, such as weaving in and out of traffic. You get angry when you perceive you're being threatened, challenged, or questioned. If someone looks at you the wrong way, you're ready for a fight, never for flight.

As Garbarino noted, you've developed a repertory of aggressive behaviors to pull out when you feel threatened. You've concluded that aggression is a successful way to get what you want.

But it's exhausting to be angry all the time—for you, for your family, for everyone who must tiptoe around you. Your anger also contributes to depression.

My hope is that by the end of the book, you will have discovered why you feel so angry and take the opportunity to do something about it.

REFLECTION EXERCISE:

To what extent are you easily angered?

| never | rarely | sometimes | usually | always |

4. YOU'RE NOT SURE WHAT HEALTHY MALE BEHAVIOR LOOKS LIKE

When I joined the Army after quitting high school, I was assigned to the 82nd Airborne Division at Fort Bragg, North Carolina. I rose to the rank of Specialist 4 in the minimum time and became overly prideful about it.

When I didn't make Sergeant in the minimum time, I started bugging my Master Sergeant every few days about when I would be promoted. Finally, he sat me down and said, "Son, let me give you some advice. The more you pester me, the less motivated I am to promote you."

My launch into manhood was awkward. My situational awareness was virtually nonexistent. I didn't have good boundaries. My emotional intelligence was stunted. I floundered. No one had taken me under their wing and mentored me about what it looks like to be a man.

Perhaps you also were not fathered, mothered, mentored, and coached about what it means to be a man. You were unprepared for adulthood because your parents didn't equip you to become independent.

From college and career advice, to finding something you can do well, to dating and sex education, all the way to personal hygiene—you weren't sure what normal, healthy male behavior looks like.

Still today, you don't know what you don't know, but you put up a good front. You keep guessing at what healthy manhood looks like. Sometimes you get it right, but you're just as likely to get it wrong. You're baffled by your own behavior, and you tend to blame yourself for not knowing what only a more experienced man could teach you.

You feel socially awkward and insecure. You sabotage your relationships and your career. You can be intense, coming on too strong around others. You say things that should be left unsaid. You make people uncomfortable, and you don't know why. You are fragile but afraid to appear weak by asking for help.

You find it difficult to rise above your circumstances. You want to be steady like a thermostat, not up and down like a thermometer. But you don't know how to set the thermostat.

The impacts of not understanding healthy male behavior have been far reaching—for example:

- Have you settled who you are and what your life is all about?
- Do you know what a good marriage looks like?
- Do you know what it takes to be a good dad?
- Do you know how to find work that is satisfying and honors God?
- Do you feel your life is going somewhere?
- Do you feel other people are "for" you?
- Do you feel accepted regardless of how you perform?
- Are you generally happy and upbeat about life?

The good news is that it's not too late. I want to help you understand and feel empowered to embrace normal, healthy male behavior.

REFLECTION EXERCISE:

How often do you feel like you know what healthy male behavior is in a given situation?

never	rarely	sometimes	usually	always

So far, we've touched on four of the nine characteristics of broken boys. Pause here so you can reflect on what you've read so far and how it relates to your own wounds.

REFLECTION AND DISCUSSION

1. With which of the nine characteristics listed on page 41 do you most identify? (Choose as many as apply.)

2. To what extent do you struggle to believe that people really care about you? Give an example.

3. Do others accuse you of being oversensitive or taking things too personally? Give an example.

4. Is there something that routinely triggers your anger?
    How are you able to control it?

5. Is there a particular area of your life where you struggle
    to understand what normal, healthy male behavior
    looks like? If there is, who is someone you could ask
    to take you under his wing in that area and show you
    the ropes?

UNDERSTANDING YOUR WOUNDS—PART 2

NOT EVERY CHARACTERISTIC YOU EXHIBIT is exclusively the result of childhood wounds, but the nine we're exploring strongly correlate to growing up in a dysfunctional home. Here are the descriptions of the remaining five.

5. YOU'RE INSECURE AND NEED CONSTANT REASSURANCE

You may be a terrific teacher, leader, mentor, husband, father, friend, or spiritual father, but you lack confidence. You may excel at your work, but you still have nagging doubts about your abilities.

Your insecurity compels you to let people take advantage of you. Often you are loyal to a fault. Someone can betray you, and you still will bend over backward to give them repeated chances far beyond what they deserve. But your motive isn't charity; it's the fear of loss.

This also means you tend to be a people pleaser. You don't like to rock the boat. You try to keep the peace and make everyone happy. You are fearful of hurting someone's feelings and equally concerned that someone will be irritated by something you say or do. You avoid confrontation at all costs.

Because you have a strong desire for people to like you, you can be grandiose. You're not above name-dropping, showing off your possessions, or exaggerating your past to improve the way people see you. You lie when the truth would work just as well. As a young man, I lied to my friends that I had orders to go into combat, but my Master Sergeant came and personally took me off the plane just before takeoff because he wanted me to keep working for him. It never happened, but I felt more important when I told the lie. So I did—for a decade.

If one or both of your parents were authoritarian, you grew up under high demands for conformity and outward obedience. You were yelled at or spanked (sometimes in anger) when you got it wrong, but you weren't affirmed when you got it right. It was not a safe, flourishing environment. You lacked social support and emotional security.

It's hard to grow secure roots in angry, unsupportive soil. As a result, you have low self-esteem, unsure if you even like yourself. Everyone has self-doubts, but yours are exaggerated. Frequently you feel unworthy of love, respect, or others believing in you. You're prone to sadness or even depression, and contentment is elusive. There's always one more thing you need to do to be good enough. It's hard for you to just "be."

In relationships, you're either too shy or too aggressive. When you feel like someone thinks they're better than you, it's really that you don't think you are as good as them. You deflect praise because you don't think you're worthy or deserve it, yet you crave reassurance. You constantly seek approval and positive feedback to let you know that you're okay. This is exhausting for you but also for your loved ones.

Encouragement is the food of the heart, and every heart is hungry. But yours is exceptionally hungry. You cling to any words of encouragement or affirmation the way a drowning man clings to a life raft. All that will change as your wounds start to heal.

REFLECTION EXERCISE:
To what extent do you feel insecure and look for constant reassurance that you're okay?

never	rarely	sometimes	usually	always

6. YOU HAVE DRAMATIC MOOD SWINGS AND DON'T KNOW WHY

Once I was speaking at a men's event, and the worship leader disappeared when I spoke, only to reappear when I was done. I assumed the worst and felt deflated. The next day he apologized and said his son had called needing some fatherly advice, as he was intending to propose to his fiancée that night. I had completely imagined the slight.

In the same way I did, you *look* for ways to create the least favorable explanation. You're still angry about what happened to you as a child, and you dread feeling that way again. That leads to overthinking your circumstances, then overreacting based on what might happen.

You're mercurial. You lack control over your emotions. You can swing from anger to sadness to fear to good thoughts and then back again to bad thoughts—all in a matter of minutes. And you don't know why.

But your baseline mood is most often sad, mad, bad, bitter, self-conscious, or irritable. When you're in such a mood, you either go looking for an argument or crawl into the nearest hole to avoid one. In either case, you don't respond well to criticism. It throws you into a tailspin.

You keep things bottled up and get down on yourself easily. You pout when you don't get your way. But you can also pout even when you *do* get your way. Instead of being grateful for the good things that happen, you get upset about what could have gone wrong. All these reactions sabotage your relationships.

People wind you up quickly, and you wind them up quickly as well. When you're in a mood, everything is drama. Hurt feelings are a daily occurrence, and your reactions are out of proportion to the situation.

You may be having a good day, and then suddenly your spouse hesitates, a friend looks at you skeptically, or a coworker disagrees with you, and it's like someone popped your balloon. You get deflated. You feel like no one understands what you're going through, and you find it difficult to leave your past behind. We're going to work on that.

Do you have big mood swings that are difficult to explain?

never	rarely	sometimes	usually	always

7. YOU'RE EITHER "THE RESPONSIBLE SON" OR ESPECIALLY IMMATURE FOR YOUR AGE

Depending on your nature, your childhood wounds made you either as hard as a stone or as fragile as an egg.

If you were told you would never amount to anything, for example, you either played into that narrative or rejected it.

You've assumed one of two roles: (1) you're the responsible son, an overachiever determined to prove your parents were wrong, or (2) you're especially immature for your age, a chronic underachiever determined to prove they were right.

If it's the first, you may be highly disciplined, like the high-functioning alcoholic who nevertheless succeeds. You are self-sufficient and have reacted to your childhood by choosing to take responsibility and break the cycle. You might also be a protector of the weak.

As the responsible son, you feel like it's your job to keep everyone happy. You bend over backward not to let anyone down—almost to the point of enabling them—because *you've* been let down and know how it feels.

You push yourself. Some would say you're driven. You feel that if you can excel in your performance, people will need you. If you don't, they may discard you.

If you're immature for your age, having assumed the second

role, you're the champion of lost causes. You struggle to see things through, or you keep sabotaging your own success.

You're heavily dependent on others. You've reacted to your childhood by refusing to take responsibility for many or most things, including your own mistakes and sins. People can't count on you.

You lack self-control and throw temper tantrums when you don't get your own way. You want the world to revolve around you. It's as if you remain frozen in the past—you *want* to be mature, but in the heat of the moment you react childishly. Your emotions get the best of you. This may be the result of your parents enabling you to avoid accountability, but it could also be rebellion against a stifling childhood with too many rules.

My goal is to help you shed whichever dysfunctional role you've adopted so you can become the man God created you to be.

REFLECTION EXERCISE:

Do you tend to one of the extremes of being either super responsible or especially immature?

never	rarely	sometimes	usually	always

8. YOU CAN'T GET RID OF THE NEGATIVE VOICES IN YOUR HEAD

When you told your parents your dreams as a child, you didn't get uplifting, positive feedback that spurred you on. They may have even made a joke about it or scoffed and didn't believe you. You can't recall being regularly encouraged or affirmed.

Now, as an adult, you can't get rid of the negative voices in your head, even when you experience success. You're your own worst critic. And even when you're happy, you feel guilty—like you don't deserve it.

We all have a running conversation with ourselves all day long. We call it self-talk. And we need it. Self-talk is how we organize the bits and pieces of our lives into a congruent story.

But for you, the conversation is a constant reminder that you're broken and that you come from a dysfunctional background. These destructive voices make it hard for you to leave your past behind. They're on a repeating loop: *You don't belong here. You're not worthy. You don't deserve to have good things happen to you.*

You feel like you're alone in the world. You have a hard time keeping your emotions under control. You wonder why you get down on yourself so easily. You may struggle with long-term depression.

You critique your performance and beat yourself up without mercy. You are hard on yourself because you take on blame, guilt, and shame for your wounds.

Having negative thoughts is not unusual. In fact, negative thoughts are normal. But for you, they are exaggerated.

In my book *Man Alive* I teased out seven inner aches and pains men often mention when they try to put into words what they're feeling inside.[1] For you, these voices are supersized:

- "I just feel like I am in this alone."
- "I don't feel like God cares about me personally—not really."
- "I don't feel like my life has a purpose—it feels random."

- "I have these repetitive negative behaviors that keep dragging me back down."
- "My soul feels dry."
- "My most important relationships are not healthy."
- "I don't feel like I'm doing anything that will make a difference and leave the world a better place."

If these kinds of negative thoughts are first in your head before affirmation, love, peace, and joy, then you're out of alignment. By the end of this book, you will be much better prepared to take control of the conversation in your head.

REFLECTION EXERCISE:

Are you able to control the negative voices in your head?

never	rarely	sometimes	usually	always

9. YOU'VE CUT YOURSELF OFF FROM FAMILY MEMBERS EMOTIONALLY OR PHYSICALLY

If you had siblings in your dysfunctional home, your parents likely didn't parent and discipline you equally. Perhaps your siblings took advantage of your parents' blind spots, and you paid the price. Resentments built up that have never been processed.

Let me tell you what this looked like for me. My three younger brothers knew how to get under my skin. They would borrow my stuff without asking, or if they did ask, they wouldn't give it back without a hassle. I would get mad and lose my temper. Then my dad would pull off his leather belt, fold it into a strap, and whip me for lashing out at my brothers—while the offending brother sneered at me with his most wicked version of the "I got you again" smirk.

Perhaps something similar happened to you, and you still harbor resentment. You do the minimum to stay in touch, or you haven't spoken to a brother or sister in years.

In the Bible, parents treating their children unequally created epic family separations that we still talk about today. Abraham left everything to Isaac and cut Ishmael and his other children out of his will. Isaac blessed his son Jacob but not Esau, and their descendants hated each other. Joseph was the apple of his father's eye, and his brothers sold him as a slave.

As for your parents, you may hold it against them that they didn't give you the love, structure, roots, or wings you needed and deserved. They were either passive, absent, permissive, enabling, angry, demanding, or belittling. You grew up emotionally neglected or physically abandoned but didn't understand why. You vowed if you could ever get away, you would never look back or would have as little to do with them as possible.

So when you had the chance, you put distance between yourself and your family members. You withdrew—physically, emotionally, or both. In your confusion, hurt, and anger over your childhood, it was all you knew to do. You even cut yourself off from your aunts, uncles, and cousins if they reminded you of your wound.

Author and professor James Garbarino wrote in *Lost Boys* that when a little boy's soul is wounded, he will withdraw into an emotional shell and shut himself off from the world for self-preservation. As the years roll by, the shell thickens and eventually hardens.[2]

Now, many years later, you've matured as a man. The past feels further away, and the pain has faded some. Deep in your soul, you feel it's time to take steps toward reconciling these relationships. To reengage. But that pattern of withdrawal is hard to break.

As you work through the process of healing in part 2 of this book, hopefully reconciliation with your family members will be possible. But regardless, you can find the peace you've been craving.

REFLECTION EXERCISE:
To what extent have you cut yourself off from your parents and siblings?

never	rarely	sometimes	usually	always

The hopeful message of this book is that no matter how deeply you've been wounded, you can be healed and reconciled. That's the process we're going to take up in the next chapter. But first, answer these questions.

REFLECTION AND DISCUSSION

1. What is a self-doubt that makes you feel insecure?

2. Have you recently experienced a big mood swing? What were the circumstances?

3. Have you assumed the role of the responsible son or of a man especially immature for his age? Why do you think the role you identified describes you?

4. Is there a negative experience, word, thought, or voice in your head from your childhood that still torments?

5. From which of your parents and siblings are you alienated because of what happened in your childhood?

PART 2

THE PROCESS
OF HEALING

6

AN OVERVIEW OF
HOW YOU CAN HEAL

BY MY EARLY THIRTIES, my faith in God was starting to grow and strengthen. I started to ache for a relationship with my dad. At that point, we barely saw each other beyond Christmas, Thanksgiving, and the Fourth of July.

After much prayer, I invited my dad to lunch on his birthday. We had a great time, and it became an annual tradition. A few years into this, we left the cash register and walked to our vehicles, which were coincidentally parked next to each other. Without any forethought, I said, "Dad, can I give you a hug?"

Before I had time to think about it, Dad charged me like a bull. He threw his arms around me and squeezed so tight I felt like a grizzly bear had grabbed hold of me. Then he let out a long, deep, primordial groan. *Mmmmmmmm* . . . It must have lasted twenty or thirty seconds.

All I could imagine was his own deeply buried pain. His father had abandoned him when my dad was two, so he never had a father of his own to mimic. He never had a father tousle his hair, never heard a father's instruction about the ways of life. Add to that all those missed years we had not hugged.

At the end of what seemed like a brief eternity, we drew back and put our hands on each other's shoulders. He looked at me, and I looked at him. Warm, salty tears rolled down both of our cheeks.

I said, "I love you, Dad."

He said, "I love you too," and then we left. That was it.

Frankly, I'm not sure anyone could adequately explain what happened in those precious moments. Our souls were cleansed. A century of sorrows boiled to the surface in one brief instant, and the intangible pain of what could have been melted away. A taste of the shimmering glory of paradise broke upon us. God's gracious hand broke down a wall. A reconciliation took place, and I experienced unspeakable joy.

That single moment started a healing process that changed our family forever. Before that day, verbal and physical affection were unheard of. But in the years that followed, hugs and verbal expressions of love became the norm—and not just between my dad and me but for our entire family. We always greet each other and say goodbye with an embrace and "I love you."

For example, one day soon after that hug, I phoned my brother. We had not been particularly close. We were not at odds, but whatever affection we had for each other was the minimum required to be considered civil. We had chosen different paths.

However, on that day, when we started to say goodbye, for no apparent reason he said, "I love you, Pat."

What? Where in the world did that come from? I thought.

Then I said, "Well, I love you too."

"Well, I love you more than you love me!" he responded in jest.

I was thinking, *Who are you, and what have you done with my brother?*

"Nope, you don't," I replied. "I have always loved you more than you've loved me."

"That's ridiculous. I said it first!"

Then (and I'm caricaturing this a bit) I said, "Well, I don't care what you say. I love you more than you love me"—and then laughed as I quickly hung up the phone before he could say anything else!

With no fanfare, preplanning, or expectation, my family relationships began to heal. Today I believe this transformation was a supernatural work of the Holy Spirit. I've heard other men share similar stories about the transformation of their families.

THE STARTING POINT

What's it going to take for you to start healing from your childhood wounds? Healing is all about pain—acknowledging it's there, identifying where it's coming from, and then knowing how to face it, grieve, accept it, take control, and heal.

From the previous chapters, you now have a much better

understanding of where your pain is coming from—what went wrong and how that damage still affects you today.

I'm keenly aware that we've ripped open old wounds. You probably feel more fragile now than you've felt in a while, but at the same time you are also more powerful. That's because a problem properly understood is half solved.

That bear hug between my dad and me was epic. It set a healing process in motion. But it was just the beginning. Because I didn't know how to identify or put into words the concepts we're exploring in this book, my process took an additional eighteen years. Your healing can come much more quickly.

If you will stick with it and journey through the process I'm about to describe—*engaging*, not just *reading*—you can heal and take control of your life.

You are not responsible for what happened to you, but you are the only one who can do anything about it now.

STAGES OF HEALING

Healing takes place in stages, but the stages often overlap or occur out of order. Some stages may take a few weeks, others a few years. Here's an overview:

- *Overcoming denial and facing the truth:* get out of denial and acknowledge the great suffering you've had to deal with.
- *Grief:* grieve what's missing, what could have been, and work toward acceptance without overreacting in hurt and anger.
- *Forgiveness:* rethink your parents' stories and forgive.

- *Making amends:* confess any part you might have played (e.g., a difficult temperament), apologize, make amends, and ask your parents to forgive you. (Note that under no circumstances are you in any way responsible for abusive behavior against you, whether physical, emotional, or sexual—even if someone tries to manipulate you to think you share the blame.)
- *Renewal:* rehabilitate the relationship when possible.
- *Setting boundaries:* set boundaries if necessary (e.g., for toxic words still spoken to you).
- *Transformation:* intentionally and actively become a man who walks in God's power, exhibiting love, joy, peace, patience, kindness, goodness, faithfulness, gentleness, self-control, humility, integrity, gratitude, and wisdom.

There's no magical, universal, or rigid sequence for working through these stages. The only essential requirement for you to heal is that, at some point, you address each one of them.

For example, here's a quick timeline to demonstrate how it worked for me, organized by my age:

- **1–17:** suffered greatly as a child.
- **18:** left home and took control of my life.
- **24:** married and became a follower of Jesus.
- **25:** forgave my parents.
- **27:** pledged to break the cycle in my own family as a young father.
- **35:** heard my dad say, "I love you" for the first time and reconciled with my parents.

- **47:** learned for the first time that my dad was proud of me.
- **53:** faced the truth, overcame denial, grieved, and healed.
- **Today:** I still walk with a limp, but joyfully.
- **Today:** I help other men with childhood wounds.

Note that I forgave my parents long before I faced the truth and overcame denial. Likewise, your healing process will happen at its own pace and in its own order.

There's no need to rush it, but there's no reason to put it off any longer either. In the next chapter, we'll tackle how to overcome denial and face the truth. But first, answer the reflection and discussion questions.

AN OVERVIEW OF HOW YOU CAN HEAL

REFLECTION AND DISCUSSION

1. How would you describe the emotions you're feeling about authentically engaging with the stages of healing just described? For example, you could be any, or all, of the following: excited, hopeful, encouraged, positive, apprehensive, unsure, skeptical, fearful, anxious.

2. "You are not responsible for what happened to you, but you are the only one who can do anything about it now." Do you agree with this statement? Why or why not? If yes, what are the implications for you personally?

3. If applicable, which of the healing stages described in this chapter have you already processed? Which stage do you want to tackle next, and why?

7

EMOTIONAL AMNESIA: HOW TO OVERCOME DENIAL AND FACE THE TRUTH

WHEN I WAS IN COLLEGE, I raced motocross on weekends. My parents only came to see me race one time. That happened to be the day I had a nasty crash and was flown to the hospital in a helicopter. My parents never came to the emergency room to check on me.

You'd think that memory would be so painful it would drive me crazy. But until recently, I didn't remember them not coming to the hospital. For self-protection, I had developed a sort of emotional amnesia. Literally, for decades, I was in denial. My brain couldn't process the truth, so it chose to deactivate the memory.

Everyone compartmentalizes unpleasant memories to avoid painful thoughts, but denial goes further. Denial erases those memories from your consciousness. You can't readily access them.

Accepting that your parents failed you and that you are still under the influence of childhood wounds can be a hard pill to swallow. Who wants to dredge up and relive bad memories and feelings? Denial is the path of least resistance—less painful and difficult than trying to process what left you so broken.

However, you can't heal what you can't describe—or acknowledge. Eventually, you must face the truth head on. Hopefully, part 1 helped you more clearly recognize the ways in which you've been wounded. Now it's time to personalize what you've learned.

HARD TRUTHS, BUT WORTH IT

Facing difficult, painful, or humiliating facts from your childhood will be hard. Most worthwhile things are. I commend your bravery in tackling the truth.

But it's also going to be so liberating and soothing that you're going to feel like you're seeing things as they really are—perhaps for the first time ever.

Just as my counselor helped me demolish the fiction I had constructed to shield myself from not feeling precious to my parents, I want to help you remember what really happened—to begin processing any too-painful-to-remember experiences you've buried away.

For instance, you might conclude one or more of the following:

- "I didn't feel deeply loved or cared for."
- "I didn't know if my parents were proud of me."
- "I didn't receive enough verbal affirmation."

- "I didn't receive enough physical affection."
- "My parents didn't have enough time for me."
- "I didn't feel prepared to become a man, husband, and father."
- "I suffered from emotional or physical abuse or neglect."
- "I feel like I must perform to be accepted."
- "I'm not sure how a healthy relationship is supposed to work."
- "I still don't feel valuable and wanted."

Before we begin, I want to issue a caveat: we don't want to "overadjust" our memories either. Denial can cut both ways. That's because hurt feelings make for lopsided stories. So, be careful not to spiral into denying the *good* your parents did, because that will hinder your healing process too.

For example, I want to always remember how my father had such integrity and a wonderful, clean sense of humor. I never want to stop chuckling over some of the funny things he did.

For now, though, the goal is to face the truth about what *did* go wrong. Only then can you begin to take control of what has been controlling you.

Here's the question: What truth must you face about what your parents should have given you, the ways they failed, the wounds you carry around, and the characteristics you exhibit as a result?

What I'm proposing is that you allow yourself to remember, to feel, and even to reexperience what you have buried in your brain. This process may cause you some short-term emotional pain, but I promise it will be worth it.

Honestly, you can try to forget, put up a wall, tell yourself not to take what you missed personally, and mask your pain for years—even decades. But denial will not hide the dysfunction. And not facing the truth most definitely will not help you break the cycle.

Instead, you will find yourself in five or ten years still struggling, by degrees, with the same characteristics described in chapters 4 and 5. Until you face your demons, they will continue to haunt you.

TO HELP YOU SUCCEED

The process of facing the truth is both simple and complex. It's *complex* because we are woefully human, finite, and fragile, and while our spirits are willing, our flesh is weak. It's *simple* because just as the body is designed to heal itself, so is the brain.

Here are a handful of the actions that will best help you successfully face the truth.

Set an Overarching Goal

Affirm a positive, overarching goal for your healing process—something like "I want to be emotionally healthy, be frank with myself, and think like an adult."

For me, it's "By God's grace, I refuse to let my childhood wounds define who I will be for the rest of my life." What would be a good overarching goal for you?

Adopt "The Cycle Breaker's Credo"

The following credo captures the essence of your mission. Let me encourage you to adopt this credo now. Then, in the

Reflection and Discussion section, you will have the opportunity to sign and date your pledge.

THE CYCLE BREAKER'S CREDO

- I will not be defeated.
- I will not withdraw from life just because it is painful.
- I will confront the truth.
- I will not embrace the behaviors that started the cycle of dysfunction.
- Insofar as it is up to me, I will not run from the marriage and family responsibilities I have already assumed.
- I will engage my feelings to understand the information they give me.
- By God's grace, I will heal my childhood wounds, break the cycle, and take control of my life.

Ask God for Help

If you're lost in a forest, it's a good idea to shimmy up a tree to gain some perspective. The same idea applies when we are emotionally lost as well.

Like climbing a tree, prayer provides perspective. There's no better starting point in this process than to ask God for healing. Ask God to reveal your hidden hurts, as well as the obvious ones. The book of Psalms describes what happens when we pray for help:

> LORD my God, I called to you for help,
>   and you healed me.

You, LORD, brought me up from the realm of the dead;
you spared me from going down to the pit.

PSALM 30:2-3

Recognize Your Part

Act on what prayer reveals. It's true that God can supernaturally heal when you prayerfully call for help, but God's normal method is for you to be an active participant. For example, if you have a sore tooth, you should pray for healing, but then you should make an appointment with a dentist so God can answer your prayer in the most probable way. Personally, I find that God's Holy Spirit tends to do his best work when I do my best work.

Commit to gaining enough knowledge, experience, and wisdom that you can form a thought and then look at it objectively—like it's on a table in front of you for inspection and action.

Don't assume too much. Read. Think. Tell your story. Listen to other people's stories.

Allow Yourself to Ask Real Questions

Giving your mind permission to activate buried thoughts and experiences will begin a healthy process of recalling what happened to you. The more you ponder your past, the more you will recall. The more you recall, the more you will have additional questions.

Let me give you an example based on what I wrote down and processed when I faced the truth that my parents didn't visit when I was flown to the ER:

- Why didn't my parents come to the hospital?

- What information do the current emotions I'm feeling give me?
- My reaction now is to overreact: "I was an afterthought."
- What happened to them that made them like that?

Each time I asked a question, that exposed another, deeper question to the light:

- Why didn't my parents show interest in my career and what I was doing?
- Why didn't they ever invite our children to stay over with them? (We lived in the same city.)
- What did my mother feel? What were her struggles? How did she feel about me? Was she proud?
- What else have I compartmentalized and buried away?
- Does this help explain why I quit high school?
- Did this feed my anger issue?
- Is this why I still take it so hard when people let me down?
- Could this be why I had such limited interest in my mother's and father's families?

You may or may not be able to come up with good answers right away—or ever, but either way you will no longer be denying what turned you into a broken boy.

NOW IT'S YOUR TURN

Now you try it. Write down the truth you've been denying and need to face. Start by picking one painful memory—one you've tried to put out of your mind. Instead, mull it over. As you do, questions will start coming to you. Don't repress them. Instead, write them down—like I did in the example. Use the lined space provided at the end of this chapter, a separate journal, or an electronic device, and write down your feelings, memories, and thoughts. As Francis Bacon noted, "Writing maketh an exact man."

When you're satisfied, move on to the other painful memories you've been able to recall so far.

If your memories lead to unfamiliar or powerful emotions, allow yourself to experience them. As my counselor advised, don't try to manufacture them, but don't try to control or suppress them either.

You will need to complete this exercise before moving on to the next chapter. The purpose of writing is to hasten the death of denial and the beginning of grief.

Here are three suggestions to help you get started:

1. What do you most identify with from chapters 3, 4, 5, and 6?
   - Is it a lack of love, structure, roots, or wings?
   - Is it parents who were passive, absent, permissive, enabling, angry, demanding, or belittling?
   - Is it that you don't feel like people care, you are overly sensitive, easily angered, guessing at what's normal, insecure, subject to mood swings, feeling overly responsible or irresponsible, unable to silence the negative voices in your head, or cutting yourself off from family?
2. Refer to the notes I scribbled to myself when I was finally able to accept that my parents had failed me (see

"The Beginning of Grief" section on pages 18-19).
Do these notes stir anything inside you? Do your
experiences resonate with mine?

3. Use the questions in the section "Allow Yourself
to Ask Real Questions" (pages 82-83) to prompt
questions you may have. Are your questions anything
like mine?

THE TRUTH I NEED TO FACE

FROM BROKEN BOY TO MENDED MAN

86

REFLECTION AND DISCUSSION

1. To what extent has "emotional amnesia" kept you from facing the truth about your childhood wounds? Give an example of a truth you kept buried and how it has affected your life.

2. Did writing "The Truth I Need to Face" help you describe, acknowledge, and face the truth about what happened to you? What is your biggest takeaway?

3. Write down the positive, overarching goal you want to make about overcoming denial and facing the truth:

_____

_____

_____

4. Pledge, sign, and date the following credo:

THE CYCLE BREAKER'S CREDO
- I will not be defeated.
- I will not withdraw from life just because it is painful.
- I will confront the truth.
- I will not embrace the behaviors that started the cycle of dysfunction.
- Insofar as it is up to me, I will not run from the marriage and family responsibilities I have already assumed.
- I will engage my feelings to understand the information they give me.
- By God's grace, I will heal my childhood wounds, break the cycle, and take control of my life.

_____ (signature)

_____ (date)

8

HOW TO GRIEVE WHAT
SHOULD HAVE BEEN

I WAS DOING "OKAY" before I discovered I had been emotionally neglected. Once my counselor helped me face the truth, that all changed. Grief hit hard.

> **grief**, *noun*,
> keen mental suffering or distress over affliction or loss;
> sharp sorrow; painful regret.[1]

In this chapter, I want to help you understand grief, and then I want to help you grieve.

Something was taken from you. You didn't have the childhood you wanted, deserved, and should have experienced. You have been afflicted. You feel the loss deeply. That's grief.

Now that you've faced the truth, you need to grieve what went wrong. Grieving is the opposite of denial. If denial is trying to forget, grieving is trying to remember. Denial stores up pain; grieving lets it out.

During my eight counseling sessions, I wrote my wife, "Patsy, this counseling and reading is helping me accept who I am, mourn the 'ideal' that never was, and pave the way to be a better husband, father, and friend. Yes, I feel sad, but immensely joyful about learning that, as my counselor said, I came by this honestly."

Like me, you also came by certain characteristics honestly. You didn't deserve your early wounds. You are not responsible for what happened to you as a child. It's not your fault. But now as a man, you *are* responsible for what happens in the future.

Self-care, however, comes first. If you take care of your own healing first, the process of healing relationships can be an act of joy from a place of strength rather than merely an exercise in self-discipline. It's the principle of putting on your own oxygen mask before assisting others—like the safety instructions before takeoff on your most recent flight.

In this chapter, you have one thing to do: let it out. There is no one right way to grieve, but good grieving will include knowing what to expect, pouring out your heart to God, talking to someone you trust, and yes, probably having a good cry.

KNOW WHAT TO EXPECT

Grief and grieving are in the DNA of human experience. However, grief over father or mother wounds is in a league of its own.

The stages or phases of grieving—anger, sadness, mood swings, outbursts, withdrawal, tears, depression, bargaining, acceptance—can't be charted on a graph. In fact, sometimes you'll feel several of these emotions at the same time. Everything hurts.

Expect your grief to come in unpredictable waves—sometimes as a ripple, sometimes as a swell big enough to swamp your boat, and sometimes as a rogue wave out of nowhere that turns you into a wreck.

For example, when I started my career, many of the young guys I spent time with already knew each other from college. They had developed deep relationships. While I was clueless, they seemed to have a grasp of the bigger picture. Their parents had prepared them for their careers and opened doors for them to get ahead. Often, when I saw them interacting, a wave of grief would leave me feeling sad over what I had missed out on.

Or take the tsunami of grief that overwhelmed a friend of mine whose loving father nevertheless let alcohol wreck their family:

When my dad died, I had so many complex feelings around it, but I also had a lot *to do* for the funeral, his finances, etc.—all while taking care of my own child plus another on the way. It kept me busy and didn't leave a lot of time for grief. On the day of the funeral, during setup, I was coming out of the bathroom when I heard the pianist practicing a song my dad had often played on the piano. I froze. The weight of the world fell on me. I stood outside of the bathroom door, tucked around the corner, and cried—for what was, what could have been, what should have been, and everything in between.

The good news is that grief shrinks over time. Just as your body will restore a broken bone with proper medical attention, so your soul will restore a broken heart over time, as you apply the Bible's healing process. There's no need to rush, but no reason to delay either. The sooner you grieve, the sooner you'll heal.

POUR OUT YOUR HEART TO GOD

The foundation of this book is that the Bible prescribes a process for healing childhood wounds that has been in constant, successful use for thousands of years. Certainly, the Bible doesn't sugarcoat the truth that parents create childhood wounds.

It is also full of grief and grieving:

- Isaac and Rebekah grieved over their son Esau's decisions (see Genesis 26:35).
- Jacob grieved the disappearance of his son Joseph (see Genesis 37:34-35).
- Judah grieved the death of his wife (see Genesis 38:12).
- Hannah grieved because she couldn't have a child (see 1 Samuel 1:15-16).
- Job grieved his physical suffering (see Job 2:12-13).
- Joel grieved when the harvest was lost (see Joel 1:10-12).
- David grieved when he was treated like an outlaw (see 2 Samuel 15:30).
- Jesus was familiar with grief and a man of many sorrows (see Isaiah 53:3).

The Bible doesn't just describe grief; it also provides a road map for grieving—like Google Maps for your soul.

Take Nehemiah, for example. When Nehemiah heard that the walls of Jerusalem were broken down, he was filled with grief. Look at what happened next:

> When I heard these things, I sat down and wept. For some days I mourned and fasted and prayed before the God of heaven.
>
> NEHEMIAH 1:4

Nehemiah paints a beautiful picture of grieving. Instead of tackling grief on his own, he poured out his heart to the God of heaven.

Through prayer and meditating on Scripture, we, too, can pour out our hearts to God. In fact—with the caveat that what I'm about to say must be *experienced* and not merely explained—thoughtful, prayerful reading of the Bible will release supernatural power into all aspects of your life, even the process of mourning.

TAKE TIME TO REFLECT

Boeing's famous test pilot, Tex Johnston, had a plaque on his office wall that read, "One test is worth a thousand opinions." Now it's time for you to test for yourself what grieving can do.

Find a quiet place where you won't be distracted for a minimum of thirty minutes. Pray through the following biblical prayers from the Psalms, which were often written in moments of suffering, sorrow, and even despair.

Read them out loud and slowly. Take time to ponder each sentiment expressed. Highlight, underline, or circle words or phrases that speak to you. If your mind begins to wander, let it. You never know what healing waters God may have for you at the end of a rabbit trail.

Once you've finished a prayer, take your time with the reflection questions. Doing so will help you authentically connect with God in ways that cannot be explained, only experienced.

How long, LORD? Will you forget me forever?
    How long will you hide your face from me?
How long must I wrestle with my thoughts
        and day after day have sorrow in my heart?
    How long will my enemy triumph over me?

Look on me and answer, LORD my God.
    Give light to my eyes, or I will sleep in death,
and my enemy will say, "I have overcome him,"
    and my foes will rejoice when I fall.

But I trust in your unfailing love;
    my heart rejoices in your salvation.
I will sing the LORD's praise,
        for he has been good to me.

PSALM 13

Reflect: What was the writer feeling as he wrote this prayer? What was he asking God? To what extent does he capture and express how you feel too?

Arise, LORD! Lift up your hand, O God.
>   Do not forget the helpless.
Why does the wicked man revile God?
>   Why does he say to himself,
>   "He won't call me to account"?
But you, God, see the trouble of the afflicted;
>   you consider their grief and take it in hand.
The victims commit themselves to you;
>   you are the helper of the fatherless.
Break the arm of the wicked man;
>   call the evildoer to account for his wickedness
>   that would not otherwise be found out.

The LORD is King for ever and ever;
>   the nations will perish from his land.
You, LORD, hear the desire of the afflicted;
>   you encourage them, and you listen to their cry,
defending the fatherless and the oppressed,
>   so that mere earthly mortals
>   will never again strike terror.

PSALM 10:12-18

Reflect: Does this prayer describe some of the anguish and grief you felt as you wrote "The Truth I Need to Face"?

When my heart was grieved
>   and my spirit embittered,
I was senseless and ignorant;
>   I was a brute beast before you.

Yet I am always with you;
    you hold me by my right hand.
You guide me with your counsel,
    and afterward you will take me into glory.
Whom have I in heaven but you?
    And earth has nothing I desire besides you.
My flesh and my heart may fail,
    but God is the strength of my heart
    and my portion forever.

Those who are far from you will perish;
    you destroy all who are unfaithful to you.
But as for me, it is good to be near God.
    I have made the Sovereign LORD my refuge;
    I will tell of all your deeds.

PSALM 73:21-28

Reflect: What hope is expressed in this prayer? Are you feeling that hope? Did praying this prayer release some of the pressure bottled up inside you?

TALK TO SOMEONE YOU TRUST

In my vocation, I listen to many men in one-on-one conversations. When men feel stuck, I always ask them if they have a friend or small group with whom they can share what's really going on. I cannot remember a single instance of a hurting man ever saying yes.

In his book *Walden*, Henry David Thoreau wrote, "The mass of men lead lives of quiet desperation." Isolation magnifies that desperation. Loneliness makes us especially vulnerable to the voices in our heads that spew out shame, false guilt, hatred, and inferiority.

If that's you, who can blame you for holding all that in? I know that I was, and still am, embarrassed about some of my emotions. But to heal properly, I needed to tell someone what I was going through, and the same is true for you.

Sharing your emotions as you grieve is a standard, indispensable part of the healing process. Whatever is stirring inside you, share it with your spouse or partner, best friend, family member, small group, or, depending how deep the wounds are, a counselor.

IMITATE NEHEMIAH

As soon as possible, I invite you to set aside time that will be free of interruption and distraction to imitate Nehemiah. Reread your "The Truth I Need to Face" notes, reflect on what happened when you told someone you trust, and pray the prayers of the Psalms. Pour out every thought and feeling you have and cry out to God to heal your wounds.

Don't shy away if you feel the need or desire to weep, sob, moan, groan, howl, wail, burst into tears, get moody, curse the day you were born, pound your fist on the table, or withdraw from the world for a while.

Yet, as to timing, you don't need to force or fabricate emotions if they aren't ready to come. There isn't a formula to this. But whether it's right now or later, whenever the wave of grief *does* roll in, and in whatever form, let it hit you. That's your only task for this stage of healing.

WRITE YOUR OWN PRAYER

Finally, express your grief to God by writing a prayer of your own to cap off the gusher of grief you've been living with.

There's no right or wrong way to grieve. Your prayer doesn't have to be perfect, or the last one you write. But as the saying goes, a journey of a thousand miles starts with the first step.

You can be raw in your prayer—in fact, you *should* be raw. Honestly tell God in writing how you feel—even if that includes anger at him for allowing your wounds to happen in the first place. And ask him for help to heal.

_____

_____

_____

_____

_____

_____

_____

_____

_____

_____

_____

_____

_____

_____

_____

_____

_____

_____

_____

This is what it looks like to grieve and mourn what should have been. Getting grief out makes space for healing to come in. In a sense, it's the act of exhaling. In the next chapter, we'll focus on inhaling.

REFLECTION AND DISCUSSION

1. What has been your biggest pain point when thinking about your childhood wounds?

2. In what way did you sense God's presence as you grieved over "The Truth I Need to Face" notes and prayed through the psalms?

3. What is the main point of the prayer you wrote out, and why?

4. How released from your grief do you feel right now? How would you explain it to a friend?

9

HOW TO FIND REST FOR YOUR SOUL

IF THE FRATERNAL ORDER OF BROKEN BOYS held a convention and a stranger walked in, they would conclude, "This is the most diverse group of men ever assembled in one place."

We are weak and strong, rich and poor, straight and gay, conservative and liberal, leaders and followers, introverts and extroverts, and every color of skin. We are strong faiths, weak faiths, lost faiths, and no faiths. No category of men is immune to childhood wounds.

But if that same stranger could see the leftover pain we each carry in our souls, they would instead say, "Wow, I've never seen a more similar group of men."

Let's take stock of where you may be in the healing process at this point. You have faced the truth. You are no longer in denial. You have grieved what was taken from you. What's your next step?

Did you know that all successful recovery programs address spiritual needs? The granddaddy of them all, Alcoholics Anonymous (AA), is the universally accepted gold standard for recovery programs, and it is also easily applicable to healing childhood wounds. AA is famous for creating the twelve-step program. Notice that God is mentioned in half the steps:

1. We admitted we were powerless over alcohol—that our lives had become unmanageable.
2. Came to believe that a Power greater than ourselves could restore us to sanity.
3. Made a decision to turn our will and our lives over to the care of God as we understood Him.
4. Made a searching and fearless moral inventory of ourselves.
5. Admitted to God, to ourselves, and to another human being the exact nature of our wrongs.
6. Were entirely ready to have God remove all these defects of character.
7. Humbly asked Him to remove our shortcomings.
8. Made a list of all persons we had harmed, and became willing to make amends to them all.
9. Made direct amends to such people wherever possible, except when to do so would injure them or others.
10. Continued to take personal inventory and when we were wrong promptly admitted it.
11. Sought through prayer and meditation to improve our conscious contact with God as we understood Him, praying only for knowledge of His will for us and the power to carry that out.

12. Having had a spiritual awakening as the result of these Steps, we tried to carry this message to alcoholics, and to practice these principles in all our affairs.[1]

The Alcoholics Anonymous Big Book says, "Remember that we deal with alcohol—cunning, baffling, powerful! Without help it is too much for us. But there is One who has all power—that One is God. May you find Him now!"[2]

Childhood wounds are every bit as cunning, baffling, and powerful as alcohol. Just as AA and every other effective recovery program includes seeking God's help, so must we. Let me illustrate by explaining how God helped me.

MY RETURN TO SANITY

In my late teens and early twenties, I started seeking rest for my soul. At the time I didn't fully understand what I was looking for. I tried religion, poetry, education, love, friendships, self-discipline, self-help literature, theater, sports, fraternities, and more. All of it left me empty.

Then I met Patsy. There was something different about her. She had the peace I was looking for. Patsy wanted to marry a Christian. When she explained her faith, I misunderstood what she meant. To be fair, I thought I already was a Christian. I had grown up in a church. But truth be told, I only knew enough about Jesus to be disappointed in him.

When I answered Patsy's questions about my faith, I could see my answers were off. Before long, I stopped answering and instead would ask her a follow-up question to figure out what she was hoping I would say. Then I would tell her what she wanted to hear. It would be fair to say I tricked her into thinking I shared her views. I loved her and wanted to spend my life with her.

However, within a few weeks after our wedding, it became clear we needed to resolve an ambiguity of terms about what it meant to be a Christian. You see, I was committed to a set of Christian values, and I viewed faith as a *task*. She, on the other hand, was committed to a person, Jesus, and she understood faith as a *relationship*.

One morning, desperate to understand the difference, I walked into a church with my wife. Without coming on too strong, a few men introduced themselves. They had obviously thought through the answers to questions like "When a young man brings his new wife to church, why does he do that? What problem is he trying to solve? What does he need from us? How can we give it to him?"

That small group of men accepted me as I was. They took me to lunch. They invited my wife and me to dinner. The pastor talked about how much God loves us. I was invited to men's events where men shared their faith stories. They didn't violate the process of relationships. They didn't push. They didn't judge. But they did model to me the love of Jesus. Those men had what I wanted, and I found it irresistible.

Finally, the difference sank in: faith is not a task we perform to make God happy but a relationship with a person. I embraced a relationship with Jesus, and my life was transformed. Some changes were instant, and others are still in progress. But since I made that choice, I've always had rest in my soul. In fact, several decades later, I can honestly say that my worst day with Jesus has been infinitely better than my best day without him.

Have you found that kind of rest yet? Or are you still searching? You can experience a deep sense of contentment and peace that doesn't depend on your circumstances. Let me show you how.

FINDING REST IN A RELATIONSHIP

When Americans have a problem, we tend to ask, "How can I fix this?" I've been told that in Asia they tend to ask a different question: "What relationships do we need to put into place to solve this problem?"

Healing your childhood wounds is a problem you can try to "fix," or you can ask, "What relationships should I seek to solve this problem?"

What we all want in life more than anything else is that one person—and we don't need more than one—who, knowing all our broken parts, still adores us and thinks we hung the moon. That will be enough.

It is a beautiful feeling when, without fear of judgment, you can openly share what happened to you with someone who really cares. It's wonderful to be accepted and loved, in spite of your wounds. As the philosopher Simone Weil said, "Attention is the rarest and purest form of generosity."

Jesus can be that person for you, as he is for me. He can deal gently with you because he, too, has suffered and understands our weakness:

He was despised and rejected by mankind,
      a man of suffering, and familiar with pain.
ISAIAH 53:3

He is able to deal gently with those who are ignorant
and are going astray, since he himself is subject to
weakness.

HEBREWS 5:2

We do not have a high priest [Jesus] who is unable
to empathize with our weaknesses, but we have one
who has been tempted in every way, just as we are—
yet he did not sin.

HEBREWS 4:15

Jesus was the incarnation of God in a human body so that
we might comprehend him better:

The Son is the image of the invisible God.

COLOSSIANS 1:15

In Christ all the fullness of the Deity lives in bodily
form.

COLOSSIANS 2:9

The Son is the radiance of God's glory and the exact
representation of his being.

HEBREWS 1:3

Jesus answered, "Anyone who has seen me has seen
the Father."

JOHN 14:9

As the Son of God, Jesus invites all of us to come to him and find rest for our souls:

> When he saw the crowds, he [Jesus] had compassion on them, because they were harassed and helpless, like sheep without a shepherd.
>
> MATTHEW 9:36

> [Jesus said,] "Come to me, all you who are weary and burdened, and I will give you rest. Take my yoke upon you and learn from me, for I am gentle and humble in heart, and you will find rest for your souls. For my yoke is easy and my burden is light."
>
> MATTHEW 11:28-30

> [Jesus said,] "As the Father has loved me, so have I loved you. Now remain in my love."
>
> JOHN 15:9

HOW GOD FEELS ABOUT YOU

I am at heart a Bible teacher. I've spent decades curating a file of notes to help me prepare messages for the men in our weekly Bible study. One of those notes is a section of Bible verses I call "How God Sees My Men." God sees you fully, knows you completely, and loves you personally. More than that, God *wants* to bring you healing:

> No one is cast off
>   by the Lord forever.

Though he brings grief, he will show compassion,
　　so great is his unfailing love.
For he does not willingly bring affliction
　　or grief to anyone.

LAMENTATIONS 3:31-33

A bruised reed he will not break,
　　and a smoldering wick he will not snuff out.

ISAIAH 42:3

Do not forget this one thing, dear friends: With the
Lord a day is like a thousand years, and a thousand
years are like a day. The Lord is not slow in keeping
his promise, as some understand slowness. Instead
he is patient with you, not wanting anyone to perish,
but everyone to come to repentance.

2 PETER 3:8-9

This is good, and pleases God our Savior, who wants
all people to be saved and to come to a knowledge of
the truth.

1 TIMOTHY 2:3-4

I take no pleasure in the death of anyone, declares the
Sovereign LORD. Repent and live!

EZEKIEL 18:32

In the same way your Father in heaven is not willing
that any of these little ones should perish.

MATTHEW 18:14

Jesus is safe. You can completely let down your guard and fully relax. He will save you from the soul-crushing weight of your childhood wounds.

The most important note in my message preparation file is this: *What one idea, fully understood and truly believed, would change everything?*

For broken boys, the big idea is that a relationship with Jesus can give you the rest for your soul that no amount of human effort will ever be able to provide.

Maybe a relationship with Jesus would be new to you, or maybe you made a profession of faith in him at a younger age. Maybe your faith is strong, or maybe you've strayed. In either case, if you like this idea and want to affirm, reaffirm, or renew a relationship with Jesus, here is a prayer you can recite to express your desire. You can pray silently or out loud, or adapt it into your own words. What matters most is the desire of your heart:

Jesus, I am tired, weary, broken, bruised, fragile, harassed, and helpless. My soul cries out for rest. Have compassion on me. As an act of faith, even if it is tiny, even if I still have many doubts, I come to you for rest. I choose to submit myself to you and learn from you. Please forgive my sins. I want a relationship with you as both my Savior and my Lord. Please be the relationship that heals my childhood wounds. Take control and grant me rest for my soul, both in this life and for eternity. Amen.

If you prayed this prayer, welcome (or welcome back) to the Kingdom of Christ. Answer the reflection and discussion questions, and then let's see how you can go about forgiving your parents.

REFLECTION AND DISCUSSION

1. What is the most impactful thought, insight, or epiphany you had when reading the AA Twelve Steps (see pages 104-105)?

2. How have you understood Christian faith—as a task and commitment to a set of values or as a relationship with Jesus?

3. Did you pray to affirm or reaffirm your faith? If yes, is your soul at rest? Explain your answer. If not, who can you talk to about your reservations?

10

HOW TO FORGIVE
YOUR PARENTS

ONE THANKSGIVING EARLY IN OUR MARRIAGE, my wife and I went to my parents' home to celebrate my brother's safe return from war. All three of my brothers, our mom and dad, my wife, and I gathered around the dinner table for the first time in many years.

Our tradition growing up was to pray before meals, "God is good, God is great, and we thank him for this food. Amen." It was a rote prayer—sincere, but often said in a hurry.

On this Thanksgiving, Dad said the blessing. Instead of zipping through the usual prayer, he bowed his head and said reverently, "Dear God, Mom and I just want to start by saying thank you . . ." That was as far as he got. He started heaving with tears, excused himself, and rushed into their bedroom.

I followed and asked, "Dad, what's wrong? Are you okay? What just happened?"

After he regained his composure, he said, "I'm okay. It's just that your mother and I never thought we would ever see our four boys together again in the same room."

Something softened in me that day, and because I had been freely forgiven by God for my sins, I silently forgave my parents for theirs. I never felt the need to discuss how they had hurt me any further.

It may not be the same for you. If you're regularly being impacted by bad feelings toward a parent, such as resentment or bitterness, you may need to have a difficult conversation before you can proceed in your healing process.

I will walk you through what this conversation might look like in chapters 12 and 13, "How to Rebuild Your Relationships (or Set Boundaries)." However, to give that conversation the highest likelihood of success, you should unconditionally forgive them first.

For example, Mike's father dreamed about having a son who would play football. That dream shattered when Mike was born without the tips of a few fingers. On Mike's sixteenth birthday, his dad told him, "The day you were born was the worst day of my life." The damage was done, and his father has never shown remorse for his comment. When Mike told me his story over dinner, he said it still hurts years later when he thinks about it, but the pain doesn't possess him the way it once did. Mike chose to forgive him, and it set Mike free from bondage to the sins of his father.

At first blush, that may seem overly simplistic or even impossible, but let me explain.

THE BIGGER PICTURE

No one can change what happened. Our parents are responsible for how they wounded us, whether they knew what they were doing or not.

Many times I've wondered, *Why didn't my parents rescue me?* I think the simplest answer is they didn't know how. This is just one more reason I think my father and mother would want me to work through our family's experiences with you. What happened to their four boys should never have happened.

Maybe your parents are living; maybe not. Maybe you have a good relationship with them; maybe not. Maybe your relationship is civil; maybe not. Whatever your relationship with your parents is like, the elephant in the room is forgiveness.

Forgiving is not dismissing what they did or pretending that your wounds never happened. After all, there would be no need for forgiveness unless somebody had done something wrong.

Forgiveness is making a conscious decision to pardon your parents in spite of what they did. It's an act of grace, not because they deserve it. And it's central to getting out of the mental bondage you feel.

You're not sweeping your parents' sins under the rug, nor are you saying that forgiveness alone will erase the years of hurt.

But without forgiveness, the future of your relationship with your parents will look no different from the past.

THE UNIQUENESS OF BIBLICAL FORGIVENESS

One day Jesus explained how to handle sin, after which the apostle Peter asked him, "Lord, how many times shall I forgive my brother or sister who sins against me? Up to seven times?" (Matthew 18:21).

What makes Peter's question so interesting is that Jewish rabbis at that time required forgiving a person for the same sin up to three times. After that, you didn't have to forgive them anymore. It was the original three-strikes law.

But Jesus answered Peter, "I tell you, not seven times, but seventy-seven times" (Matthew 18:22).

Jesus wasn't just telling people to count higher. Instead, he was using hyperbole to do away with the "three strikes and you're out" rule altogether. The Jesus rule? However often someone sins against us, we are to forgive them.

Notice that Peter didn't ask, nor did Jesus answer, "When someone comes to you, bows down and bends their knee, confesses their sin, tells you how sorry they are, and begs forgiveness, how many times should I forgive them?"

Jesus teaches *unilateral* forgiveness. We are to forgive people when they sin against us—whether they're sorry or not, and whether they've asked to be forgiven or not.

In the Sermon on the Mount, Jesus taught his disciples how to pray:

Our Father in heaven,
hallowed be your name,
your kingdom come,
your will be done,
    on earth as it is in heaven.
Give us today our daily bread.
And forgive us our debts [sins],

as we also have forgiven our debtors [those who have
sinned against us].
And lead us not into temptation,
but deliver us from the evil one.

MATTHEW 6:9-13

Of all the lofty thoughts compressed into what we call
the Lord's Prayer, note that the first idea Jesus expanded is
forgiveness:

For if you forgive other people when they sin against
you, your heavenly Father will also forgive you. But if
you do not forgive others their sins, your Father will
not forgive your sins.

MATTHEW 6:14-15

Jesus does *not* teach that an apology is necessary. He teaches
that we are to forgive regardless.

Perhaps you are walking around angry, holding a grudge,
harboring resentment, or stewing in bitterness because your
parents wronged you. When you refuse to forgive them, your
fellowship with God is broken. Jesus is clear: if you won't forgive
your parents, your Father in heaven won't forgive you.

Notice that we are not yet discussing reconciliation.
Forgiveness and reconciliation are related, but they are two
different things. For example, an apology *is* usually needed
before you can experience genuine reconciliation (more on this
in chapters 12 and 13).

The uniqueness of biblical forgiveness is that even when

your parents don't deserve it, are no longer alive, or show no remorse, you can still forgive them.

FORGIVING THEM HEALS YOU

Why does it matter? When you don't forgive, you are the one who suffers most. Accumulated unforgiveness is like a festering wound that gets infected when not treated.

Nelson Mandela, who endured apartheid and eventually became president of South Africa, remarked, "Resentment is like drinking poison and then hoping it will kill your enemies."

Until you forgive, you will continue to suffer.

Forgiveness is about releasing *your* mind, heart, soul, and spirit from bondage.

Jesus Is Our Role Model

The essence of Christ's message is that, because of his love, no matter what someone has done, they can be forgiven.

Jesus didn't come just to forgive and save "the good people." On the contrary, Mark 2:17 states, "Jesus said to them, 'It is not the healthy who need a doctor, but the sick. I have not come to call the righteous, but sinners.'"

Good thing, too, because we're all included in the sick. Let's be honest. You and I are both three-strikers who could never earn or deserve Jesus' forgiveness. We have all done things that seem unforgivable. Yet he freely offers us forgiveness anyway—without any payment or cost.

The same applies to your parents. No doubt your parents are three-strikers too. But because of God's love for them, no matter what they have done, they can be forgiven.

Forgiving Your Parents

God didn't need you to love him before he extended you forgiveness. "God demonstrates his own love for us in this: While we were still sinners, Christ died for us" (Romans 5:8).

In the same way, you don't need your parents to love you before you can extend forgiveness to them. We can forgive our parents when they don't deserve it because God forgives us when we don't deserve it.

Here's the bottom line: God loves your parents just as much as he loves you. No matter what your parents have done, you can and should forgive them right now. Unilaterally. Without regard to whether they're sorry. Forgiving your parents will only make your life better, not worse.

Mark Twain reportedly said, "Forgiveness is the fragrance the violet sheds on the heel that crushed it." Wouldn't it speak volumes to others if you were known for the ease with which you're able to forgive?

"I DON'T KNOW HOW"

Reggie's father was AWOL when he was growing up. When Reggie was in his forties, his father realized the error of his ways and apologized. He asked Reggie, "Can you forgive me?"

Reggie replied honestly, "I don't know how."

Can you relate to Reggie's uncertainty? The good news is it's not as complicated as it may seem. You can forgive your parents, by faith, as an act of your will.

Forgiveness is volitional, not emotional. You can forgive in your brain by faith and then give your emotions time to catch up. The emotional catchup could take days, months, or even years. We'll explore this further.

At this point, however, forgiveness is something between you and God, not between you and your parents. You can tell God you forgive your parents, praying along these, or similar, lines:

God, thank you for helping me face the truth, get out of denial, and grieve what could have been. Now, by faith, as an act of my will, I forgive my parents their sins, as you have forgiven me for my sins. I do this unilaterally, without regard to how they might respond. I forgive them so that they can get on with their lives (if living) and so that I can get on with mine. Show me how to take responsibility for my own sins, as you show them how to take responsibility for theirs. I realize reconciliation and forgiveness are different. However, my forgiveness is unconditional. In Jesus' name I pray, amen.

For you, this may seem like a hurdle that's too big to get over. No one can tell you it will be easy, but I assure you that nothing is impossible for the Holy Spirit. Let me give you an example.

HOW THE IMPOSSIBLE BECOMES POSSIBLE

My friend Sean never imagined he could forgive his father. Here is his story, in his own words:

My childhood was filled with psychological and physical abuse. Basically, my father beat my brother and me all the time—and he was mean about it. There was this anger and rage, and we just never knew when or why he would blow up. My parents owned a very successful business, but I think that caused them a lot of stress that they didn't know how to handle. So my brother and I always got blamed for whatever was upsetting my dad at any particular moment.

I got my nurturing from my best friend's mom. I practically lived at their house. It was a safe place. They laughed, and they played music! When I was there, it made me even more aware of how messed up my home was.

I knew I needed to get out of there as quickly as I could, so when I was old enough, I enlisted in the Air Force. I visited home as rarely as possible—I was always afraid there'd be some kind of explosion.

Then my mom got sick and was disabled for several years. My dad did nothing to help her and made it difficult for me to see her. After she died, the executor of her will called to tell me that my dad wanted nothing to do with me going forward. *No problem*, I thought, and didn't look back.

But before my mom got sick, I remember going to church one day and reading the Lord's Prayer. I had heard it many times, of course, but on this day, for whatever reason, I *really* heard it. "Forgive us our trespasses as we forgive those who trespass against us." That prayer began a long wrestling match in me.

After my mom died, I didn't see my father for seven more years. I was often driving near where he lived, but visiting the man never crossed my mind. He was dead to me. Then late one night, we were on our way home, and as we drove near my dad's house, the Holy Spirit just took over. There's no other way to explain it. God prompted me to call him.

I asked my spouse to pull over, and in the quiet darkness of the car, I found myself shaking as I dialed my dad's number. "I bet you don't know who this is," I said when he picked up. "This is your son."

After a brief exchange, I decided to go to his house. As we pulled into his long driveway, I was totally taken aback when he walked out. To be honest, I thought he might shoot me! But he said hello, formally, and we followed him inside. We had a short, stiff visit. Something was off. A week later, we got his diagnosis of dementia.

Because of his illness, I decided to help by moving him to an assisted living place a mile from our house. I took him to doctor's appointments and out for meals, but for the first year I always felt on edge. I didn't know how to interact with him. Eventually, we started being less rigid with each other. He was still a jerk, but he could also be kind, too, which was weird to see— even showing me physical affection like patting my hand.

During several years of helping to take care of him, I probably looked through thousands of photos he had saved, spanning decades. It was the craziest thing to look at photos of my childhood and see things I hadn't remembered. It makes you think—*Don't trust your memory. It may not be as complete as you believe.*

My whole life, we had been very formal with each other—no terms of endearment. I'd always called him by his first name. But in the last year of his life, somewhere along the way, I transitioned to calling him "Dad."

We never really fully reconciled, but I did forgive him. At times, I felt angry that I never got a sorry from him. I never got that *moment*. Even now, when I see a man being compassionate toward his child, I get emotional. It's still so foreign. But I realized that holding on to that anger only hurt *me*.

Six years after I went to his house that night, he had to be moved to hospice care. In his last days, I brought all the old love letters he wrote to my mom that I'd found in his house and read them to him. When I walked out of hospice for the last time, I felt the weight of it, but also a sense of peace. I looked back and said, "I tried my best. Maybe you tried yours."

Sean's father never lifted a finger to make up for the past, nor did he apologize for the wounds that turned Sean into a broken boy. Nevertheless, Sean listened to the prompting of the Holy Spirit and made a choice: *forgiveness by faith, as an act of the will*—an act that helped heal a broken boy and made the impossible possible.

Take a moment to reflect on your own story, and then take another look at the words of the prayer on page 122.

NOW WHAT?

The beautiful thing about unilateral forgiveness is that it begins to replace negative emotions with love, grace, mercy, and compassion.

Once you unilaterally forgive your parents, you may begin to see them in a different light, or to have a deeper understanding of how they became the parents they were. I'll show you how to rethink their stories in the next chapter, but first, answer the reflection and discussion questions.

REFLECTION AND DISCUSSION

1. How have you softened toward your parents, and why?

2. What might your life be like in ten years if you don't forgive your parents?

3. What makes biblical forgiveness unique?

4. Did you pray and unilaterally forgive your parents? How does that make you feel? If not, what's holding you back?

RETHINKING YOUR PARENTS' STORIES

WHEN YOU THINK ABOUT YOUR PARENTS, where do you see them on this continuum?

good-hearted	well-intentioned	dysfunctional	uncaring	toxic	evil

I gave my parents a bad rap for such a long time, eventually cutting them off, because I didn't feel like they cared about me.

But as I've matured, I've softened toward my parents. Even during the process of writing this book, I remembered how my mother used to sign birthday cards XOXO, representing kisses and hugs. That was something positive I had blocked out.

And there are other details I had forgotten. One day I recalled that she gave me a book that changed my life—*30 Days to a More Powerful Vocabulary*. I still have it. She must have recognized my love for words and wanted to help.

Here's the question for each of us: As we have positive thoughts, do we cling tightly to our old narrative, or do we make an adjustment?

To be sure, your parents are responsible for how they wounded you, whether they knew it or not. Maybe they were good people who made serious mistakes, or maybe they were uncaring, toxic, or even evil. Nothing can minimize, justify, excuse, or change that. What happened to you happened.

But what happened to *them*?

It's a worthy question. In this book, my goal is to help you unravel what happened to you, heal your childhood wounds, and break the cycle of pain. That said, unraveling what happened to your parents can illuminate what happened to *you*.

WHAT HAPPENED TO MY PARENTS

Knowing what I know now, I confess I was harsher toward my parents than they deserved. My parents' failures were not theirs alone; they didn't happen in a vacuum. Rather, my parents carried wounds and walked with limps of their own. That's not an excuse, but it does warrant some grace.

My Parents

I loved my mother, and I believe she loved me. But something was missing in her life. To this day, I don't know what. She was a private person.

My dad is a different story. I know a lot about him. Because his father left when my dad was two years old, he never felt the scratch of his father's whiskers, never played catch, never had a dad wrestle with him on the floor, and never had a dad to look up to and imitate.

The man who never hugged me or assured me of his love when I was a child had *himself* never been hugged or assured of his dad's love when he was a child.

At his funeral I shared,

When our dad was two years old, he, his mother, Mae, and his two brothers and sister were abandoned by his father. Not long after, his mom had a stroke. From that day on, she would slur her words and drag one side behind her.

Soon they lost their small farm in Hayward, Minnesota, and moved into Albert Lea to live with two of Mae's sisters. Dad's oldest brother, Harry, went to work on a bread truck before school, at the butcher shop after school, and at the filling station on weekends—at the age of ten. Dad went to work when he turned six, helping on the bread truck and delivering papers to make money. They would rise out of bed at 3:00 and had a permanent tardy slip for school.

As I've considered Dad's life and the odds against him, I have, by God's grace, come to understand this: the success and legacy of some men will be measured by how far they go. The secret of our dad's success and legacy is to look at how far he came.

When he became a man, the driving force in my dad's life was to not be like his father. Although I don't remember him ever using these exact words, he wanted to break the cycle. He knew there was an intergenerational sickness that needed to be healed.

My dad needed help. His heart was in the right place, but he had no example for manhood. What it meant to be a father was never modeled for him. He was left to guess how to be a father to my three younger brothers and me.

Our Church

Knowing they needed help and guidance, my parents took us to church. Unfortunately, when they opened the door and entered, the church was not prepared. There was no plan in place to disciple and train them to be godly parents.

When I was in the tenth grade, my parents got their feelings hurt and our family walked away from church. I was sixteen. That decision correlates with the downward spiral of my three brothers and me. Our family has still never fully recovered from that fateful decision.

I've spent a lot of time reflecting on what happened. If you asked my dad who was at fault for what happened to his family, he would take full responsibility.

But as I have come to understand the gospel of Jesus and his command to make disciples, I believe the mature Christians in that church were also culpable. Because no one grasped the sacredness of the responsibility—and opportunity—to take these two young parents under their wings and show them the ropes, they were not equipped to father or mother us well, even though they wanted to.

Why would I think those mature Christians were culpable? In part, because of what happened to me when I finally opened the door of a different church with a different group of men.

I, too, knew I needed help, so I turned to the historically designated place a man is supposed to be able to find that help. On a Sunday morning, desperate for the wisdom I lacked to be a godly man and husband, I took my wife to church.

But my experience was the opposite of Dad's. When I opened the front door, those men were ready for me. They understood the sanctity of that moment—all the spiritual forces of evil at work to prevent it and all the prayers of my wife and others to make it happen. They had a plan to take me under their wings, show me Christ's love, share his gospel, and disciple and equip me to be a godly man, husband, and father. Those men gave me a gift my dad had wanted too—desperately—but never received.

The most important part of rethinking my father's story is the realization that whatever other failings he had, he did not repeat the sins of his father. He stayed in the picture. My dad was a miracle.

REASONS TO RETHINK

There are many reasons to extend grace to your parents. For example,

- they didn't have the right temperament,
- they were not resilient,
- they had their own childhood wounds that never healed,
- they were not the gleam in their parents' eyes, or
- no one took them under their wing to model healthy, loving parenting.

It's unlikely that your parents set out to be bad parents. No one plans to fail. Maybe your parents tried, maybe they didn't, or maybe they didn't try hard enough. In any case, they didn't receive the training they needed to be good parents.

What happens when the ones who are supposed to give never received? If your parents didn't nurture you, there's a good chance it was because they weren't nurtured either. As happened to my parents, it's likely no one showed them how to provide love, structure, roots, and wings.

Remember that your parents were the product of their environment too. What demons did they have to chase—drugs, alcohol, addiction, mental illness, violent and abusive parents, a broken home? Were *their* parents passive, absent, permissive, enabling, angry, demanding, or belittling? If your mom or dad made any progress breaking the cycles they were born into, give them credit for that.

Consider that even though they let you down, your parents may have had good intentions. For example, a lot of absent parents worked long hours to make ends meet and provide for their families. That doesn't excuse them for missing important events, but it does put a different spin on it.

The more you know about your parents' stories, the more likely you are to end up with a more gracious, compassionate, and merciful view of them.

Regardless of why they let you down, though, holding your brokenness against them will not heal you. If anything, it will drag you down.

There also may be other factors involved in the wounds you carry, such as your nature, a trauma you experienced, bullying, racism, prejudice, or poverty. Not every bad thing that happens to us originates with a father or mother wound. Hence, even men who can say, "My parents were affirming" might still exhibit some of our nine characteristics.

At the end of the day, we must acknowledge that our parents—like us—are flawed humans with real feelings, and we have said things that crushed *their* spirits. As British actor and filmmaker Peter Ustinov said, "Parents are the bones upon which children sharpen their teeth." We were not perfect children, just as they were not perfect parents.

WHAT ARE YOUR PARENTS' STORIES?

Think about what you know, and don't know, about your parents' stories. Then, in the space provided, answer the question: *What happened to my parents?*

NOW WHAT?

After looking at all the reasons your parents failed you, consider that they may only have passed on to you the mistakes and sins that were passed on to them. The intergenerational transfer of dysfunctional behavior is well documented in scholarly literature.

Winston Churchill said, "Those who fail to learn from history are condemned to repeat it."[1] But now that you have considered what happened to your parents, you can break the chain.

Don't freeze your parents in a particular memory. Radio show host Erick Erickson said, "If none of us are allowed to move beyond the worst thing we've done, there's no incentive for any of us to become a better person."[2]

Extend your parents grace for their past mistakes and sins, just as you've received grace for yours.

Trying to rebuild a relationship with your parents may not seem worth the effort—and in some cases, it may not be or seem possible. But if you think you would like to give it a try, in the next two chapters we'll look at a process for reconciling and rebuilding a relationship with your parents.

REFLECTION AND DISCUSSION

1. What do you think made your parents so

_____ (fill in the blank)?

2. Based on rethinking your parents' stories, how might you adjust the way you initially saw them on the continuum?

good-hearted	well-intentioned	dysfunctional	uncaring	toxic	evil

3. Our threefold plan is to unravel what happened to you, heal your childhood wounds, and break the cycle. How has rethinking your parents' stories helped you in one or more of these three areas?

4. If it's possible, do you desire to attempt reconciling with your parents? Why or why not?

HOW TO REBUILD YOUR RELATIONSHIPS (OR SET BOUNDARIES)—PART 1

AFTER HOLDING MY PARENTS AT ARM'S LENGTH for over a decade, I felt a desire to rebuild our relationship. God had done good work in building my relationship with him. Now it was my turn to do good work in rebuilding my relationship with my parents.

I was in my early thirties, and my first step was to begin taking Dad to lunch on his birthday. That kick-started a series of wound-healing conversations throughout my thirties and forties—the most memorable being the day I first remember him saying, "I love you."

When I was forty-seven years old, I wrote on his birthday card, "Dad, I sure hope you're proud of me." After our traditional lunch, I handed him the card and carefully watched as he opened and read it. Without looking up, he said, "Well, you know I am."

That's all I ever got. But it was electric! My mind exploded with joy. Something inside me was unchained.

Your parents may be unavailable, dysfunctional beyond repair, or abusive. But if not, there's a part of you that probably wants—even aches—to have a better relationship with them. And if you feel that way, there's a high probability they feel that way too.

However, for that to happen, you must be able to talk to each other honestly about the wounds that still bother you. Talking *about* your parents is one thing; talking *to* them raises everything to a whole different level. Even the prospect of a direct conversation about pain from your childhood probably makes you feel a bit anxious, right?

I've felt it too. That's why I want to guide you through it. In this chapter, you'll assess your current situation and reflect on your attitude. Then, in the following chapter, we'll review the potential next steps, including what to do if you can't communicate.

YOUR CURRENT SITUATION

Four key factors will influence your ability to clear the air and move forward in your relationship. Let's take them one by one.

1. The Level of Dysfunction

In chapters 1–5 you unraveled what happened to you. The degree to which you were deprived of love, structure, roots, and wings can range from mild to severe. Most dysfunctional families are not evil, but some levels of dysfunction are easier to heal than others.

What were your parents like? Were they passive, absent, permissive, or enabling? Did they just not know what they were doing, like mine? Or were they angry, demanding, or belittling parents who actively tore you down? Did they abuse or neglect you?

How would you rate the level of dysfunction in your childhood family—both then and now?

low	moderate	serious	severe

If you were in the foster system or raised by relatives, rate the dysfunction of the relationships that most affected you.

2. Your Receptivity

Rebuilding a relationship with good-hearted parents who made mistakes is, of course, far different than rebuilding with selfish, mean-spirited parents who utterly failed you. As a result, your receptivity to reconciliation may be high or low.

If your parents acted out of ignorance rather than malice, you will be more receptive. But if your parents knowingly abused you, and especially if they haven't changed, you may be reluctant.

What is your level of receptivity to pursuing a better relationship with your parents?

eager	receptive	unreceptive	opposed

3. Your Parents' Receptivity

In hindsight, I have no recollection of my parents ever resisting any of my efforts to reconcile, restore, and rebuild our relationship. To be sure, I had to take the lead; they were never proactive. But they always seemed receptive and responsive to my efforts.

Perhaps your parents long to build or restore a good relationship with you but don't know how. Or it's possible they have no interest due to passivity, defensiveness, selfishness, or other reasons. The only way to know for sure is to ask them.

At this point in time, though, how receptive would you guess they are to reconciling or rebuilding?

eager	receptive	unreceptive	opposed

4. Communication Skills

Realistically, you're a broken boy because your parents or caregivers didn't have the skills or temperament to raise a healthy boy. Yet to restore a relationship, you (or a facilitator) will need strong communication skills.

Do you and your parents have the skill and maturity to engage in conversations that are both honest *and* constructive?

definitely	on some topics	unpredictable	never

If your parents aren't mature or experienced in this area, productive conversations may not be possible. But remember—if you've changed and grown, then it's possible that they have changed or can change too.

Looking at the four factors, how many of your answers are on the left end of the scale? How many are on the right? This will give you a clearer idea of what you're up against.

Next, let's reflect on the attitude that will give you the highest likelihood of making progress.

YOUR ATTITUDE

What does it mean to have a bad attitude or a good attitude? Attitude refers to your outlook—how you see the present, how you see the future, your philosophy of life, your values, your beliefs, your optimism or pessimism, whether you see the glass half full or half empty, and whether you have a positive or negative view toward people and life.

Zig Ziglar famously said, "Your attitude, not your aptitude, will determine your altitude." If your attitude in approaching your parents is to set the record straight, adjudicate the past, right a wrong, let your parents know how you *really* feel, push for an admission of guilt, or force an apology, then you will likely fail in your efforts to better your relationship.

Once again, the Bible's time-tested principles offer the highest probability of success.

The core of Jesus' teachings isn't defending your rights, placing blame, or getting even; it's *love*. Jesus said, "A new command I give you: Love one another. As I have loved you, so you must love one another. By this everyone will know that you are my disciples, if you love one another" (John 13:34-35).

Love empowers us to overlook and forgive offenses:

Above all, love each other deeply, because love covers
over a multitude of sins.
1 PETER 4:8

Hatred stirs up conflict,
    but love covers over all wrongs.
PROVERBS 10:12

Whoever would foster love covers over an offense,
    but whoever repeats the matter separates close friends.
PROVERBS 17:9

A person's wisdom yields patience;
    it is to one's glory to overlook an offense.
PROVERBS 19:11

Do everything in love.
1 CORINTHIANS 16:14

You can't love like this through willpower and determination, but you don't have to. Since love is a fruit of the Spirit,
you can love God's way by walking in the power and presence
of the Holy Spirit:

The fruit of the Spirit is love, joy, peace, forbearance
[patience], kindness, goodness, faithfulness, gentleness
and self-control.
GALATIANS 5:22-23

God didn't need you to love him for him to love you. He was the initiator:

> Dear friends, let us love one another, for love comes from God. . . . This is love: not that we loved God, but that he loved us and sent his Son as an atoning sacrifice for our sins. Dear friends, since God so loved us, we also ought to love one another. . . . We love because he first loved us.
>
> I JOHN 4:7, 10-11, 19

Likewise, your attitude toward your parents can revolve around this cathartic truth: you don't need your parents to love you for you to love them.

Love is the glue that can hold us together and the oil that can keep us from rubbing each other the wrong way. Even if your parents don't reciprocate, love can set you free from bitterness and resentment.

If you're ready, join me in making this affirmation: *I don't need my parents to love me for me to love them.*

REFLECTION AND DISCUSSION

1. What is the current level of dysfunction in your family? Explain your answer.

low	moderate	serious	severe

2. How would you rate the receptivity of you and your parents to rebuilding a relationship? Explain your answer.

eager	receptive	unreceptive	opposed

3. The Bible says our attitude should be to do everything in
    love. Did you or are you ready to make the affirmation
    *I don't need my parents to love me for me to love
    them*? Why or why not?

HOW TO REBUILD YOUR RELATIONSHIPS (OR SET BOUNDARIES)—PART 2

IN THE LAST CHAPTER, you assessed your family's current situation and receptivity to rebuilding. In this chapter, let's explore how you can communicate with your parents—and what to do if you can't.

FOR LOW TO MODERATE DYSFUNCTION

Option 1: Keep Doing What You're Doing

If the level of dysfunction in your family was—and perhaps still is—relatively mild, your first option can be to carry on as you have been.

For example, perhaps your parents both worked a lot of hours and weren't around enough. There was no violence or addiction, and their relationship was stable.

You understand what happened. So do your parents, and they have regrets. You've made progress. You communicate well with each other now. You focus on the future, not the past. You all want to break the cycle for the benefit of your children and their grandchildren.

If this sounds like your situation, you may choose to keep doing what you're doing now. You can have short, frank conversations about the issues that bother you. This was largely my approach—addressing one issue at a time, case by case, as need and opportunity presented themselves.

Option 2: Initiate a "Crucial Conversation"

Your second option is to meet for an honest conversation to clear the air.

Perhaps you've never spoken to your parents about your childhood wounds, nor they to you. It's like a family secret. If this describes your situation, there will always be a cap on how much of a trusting, loving relationship you can build with them until you address what happened to you and how it made you feel.

The book *Crucial Conversations: Tools for Talking When Stakes Are High* describes such a conversation as a discussion between two or more people, consisting of these three components:

(1) opposing opinions about a
(2) high-stakes issue and where
(3) emotions run strong.[1]

If you choose to go this route, note that it's helpful if you *and* your parents possess reasonably good communication skills.

Hopefully, at this point in your relationship, they are rarely or only occasionally passive, absent, permissive, enabling, angry, demanding, or belittling.

If they've matured to the extent that you suspect they are receptive to rebuilding your relationship further, and if you've forgiven them for how they wounded you, then a crucial conversation may be your best option.

Even if you suspect they will be mortified, humble themselves, and take responsibility, the prospect of a crucial conversation may still feel terrifying! Here are some tips to get through the awkward moments.

AWKWARD MOMENT #1: MAKING AN APPOINTMENT

I suggest you set up an appointment to meet. Formally setting a time will undoubtedly feel emotionally awkward to you—and equally awkward for your parents.

But don't overthink it. At this stage you have one, and only one, objective: to schedule a sit-down with your parents.

First, say a prayer asking God to give you success. Then schedule the meeting with a phone call. Do not do this over email or text except as a last resort. *Always* meet in person—even if you need to wait a few months or travel out of town. There can't be a meeting of the minds if the minds don't meet.

Here's a sample script you can use as is or modify to suit you:

> "Dad, this is _____. I would like to get together and talk to you and Mom. When would be a good time for us to meet for about an hour?"

Possible responses:

- "What's this about?" *Your response:* "I have some questions about my childhood. When would be a good time to meet?"
- "Can we just talk about it now?" *Your response:* "It's important enough to me that I would like to do this face-to-face. When would be a good time to meet?"
- "I don't think this is necessary" or "Now is not a good time." *Your response:* "I realize this may be stressful, but I'm in a good place right now, and I think it's important to do this in person. When would be a good time to meet?"

If your parents are still not willing to meet, you did your best. You can respond, "I understand. Please know that I have been working through how I became the man I am and have made some amazing progress. I think it would be mutually beneficial for us to spend an hour together, so please let me know if you change your mind."

At this point, you either have an appointment or you don't. If you don't, continue to hope for the best for your parents and pray for an opportunity to have this crucial conversation. But you don't need to force the issue.

AWKWARD MOMENT #2: THE FIRST FEW MINUTES

Here's a foolproof way to get your meeting off on the right foot that I learned when I needed to talk to my neighbor. Our neighbors had bought a new dog and left it on their screened porch when they went to work. Their porch was next to my writing office, and the dog barked all day to the point I couldn't concentrate.

The thought of a confrontation made me shrink, but finally I couldn't take it anymore. After a couple of weeks, I mustered up some courage and knocked on their door. When my neighbor opened the door with a big, friendly smile, I found these words coming out of my mouth: "Hi, neighbor. I love that we live next door to each other, but we need to have an awkward conversation. Would that be all right?"

Those words took all the pressure off both of us. I didn't have to fake a bunch of social pleasantries, but I wasn't grumpy or rude either. Instead, I was able to be frank, clear, and polite as I explained what was going on.

My neighbor was able to hear what I said because I didn't make a federal case out of it. Also, I listened to his side of the story and didn't challenge him or get emotional. Once we cleared the air, he agreed to keep the dog inside during the day. Problem solved. Since that day, I've never had trouble starting a crucial conversation.

Here's a similar phrase you can use or adapt in those first awkward moments when you are physically meeting with your parents: "Mom and Dad, I love you very much, but we need to have an awkward conversation. Would that be all right?"

By asking permission, you avoid appearing to force the conversation, which shows respect for them.

THE MEAT OF YOUR CONVERSATION

If you feel apprehensive about meeting, don't overthink it. You have conversations every day, and that's all you're aiming to do. Just have a conversation.

Don't go into the meeting with an agenda to adjudicate the past, force an apology, or get them to "come around." Instead, meet with a hopeful, positive attitude. Listen. Love. Respect. Clear the air.

Avoid confrontational *why* questions, such as "Why didn't you come to my games?" or "Why did you yell at me all the time?" Instead, focus on two things—*what happened to you* and *how it made you feel*:

- "When you didn't come to my games, it made me feel like you didn't care about me."
- "When you yelled at me, it made me feel afraid."

Here's the question: Can you have a positive, emotionally mature conversation in which both you and your parents can listen and speak to each other with humility and respect?

James 1:19-20 exhorts, "My dear brothers and sisters, take note of this: Everyone should be quick to listen, slow to speak and slow to become angry, because human anger does not produce the righteousness that God desires."

If you ask a question, make it clear that you genuinely want an answer. Listen without giving an overly quick reply. Don't give off the vibe that you're not really interested in understanding their side of the story.

If you want to increase your confidence prior to taking this step, read *Crucial Conversations: Tools for Talking When Stakes Are High*, which is based on twenty-five years of interviews with twenty thousand people.

FOR SERIOUS TO SEVERE DYSFUNCTION: HAVE A FACILITATED SESSION

If you've experienced serious to severe dysfunction, your wounds are likely deep and debilitating. Yet if you've now forgiven your parents, you may want to take a step toward rebuilding.

Meeting for a crucial conversation may not be wise or even possible in certain circumstances. Perhaps they've shown no remorse, don't know how to communicate like mature adults, or are so passive and indifferent that they don't appear to be that interested in your well-being.

Or perhaps you have tried to set up a meeting multiple times and they are dragging their feet. They just don't understand why you can't "grow up" or "get over it." They want to bury what you need to dig up.

Unless both you *and* your parents have good communication skills and at least some semblance of relational health and maturity, you will be better served if an experienced adviser, emotionally intelligent pastor or mutual friend, or professional counselor facilitates the conversation.

It's wise to meet with your counselor or adviser first to provide some background and an explanation of what your hopes are for the conversation. They will have suggestions about how to proceed, which you should follow.

Through counseling I realized our family dysfunction was *serious*—even though I had fantasized we were only mildly dysfunctional. Because I had misjudged our dysfunction, my parents and I never met with a counselor or pastor to facilitate honest conversations about our relationship. Now that I've been through counseling, I'm convinced we missed a huge opportunity. We would have been much better off much sooner—individually and as a family—if we had done this. I want better for you.

FOR SEVERE DYSFUNCTION: SET BOUNDARIES

If you have tried repeatedly to move toward a healthier relationship with your parents without any progress, it may not be possible at this time. Your family was, and remains, severely dysfunctional or even toxic.

Although you're trying to take responsibility for your life, your parents might prefer to ignore the past altogether and go on as if nothing happened. Whether they're refusing to cooperate with your efforts or even working against you, they just don't get it.

In these severely dysfunctional relationships, boundaries often need to be established. A boundary is a rule you set up when your parents repeatedly violate the norms of healthy parent/child relationships.

For example:

- They drink too much and then make hurtful comments—even after you've repeatedly asked them to refrain.
- When you host your parents for dinner, they openly criticize your children and speak disrespectfully to your wife.
- Your parents were AWOL when you were growing up, but now they want you to take care of them as though you owe them a debt, without addressing the past.

- You and your parents are codependent and too enmeshed in each other's lives. They ask for too much from you. You need more privacy.
- They try to control you with threats or by making you feel guilty.
- When you try to have a crucial conversation, they lose their temper and say terrible words.

No one should be able to keep violating your physical or emotional boundaries and not expect consequences—including your parents. You and you alone should be able to set and maintain your boundaries, as well as carry out the consequence if those boundaries are violated.

A boundary may be as simple as saying, "We don't serve alcohol in our home." Or it could be as drastic as "I'm responsible to protect my family from being berated and criticized. Until you will agree to stop speaking disrespectfully to my wife and criticizing our children, we need to pause getting together." You can be firm but still diplomatic.

For helpful insights on how to set boundaries, read the updated and expanded edition of *Boundaries* by Dr. Henry Cloud and Dr. John Townsend.

WHAT IF YOUR PARENTS ARE UNAVAILABLE?

If your parents are deceased or absent, you can still reconcile with them in a way that will bring you solace. You don't need to go anywhere special or follow a magic formula. However, it may help to create a sense of occasion to go where they are buried (if they are deceased) or another place of significance, if possible.

Tell them about the things you've realized and worked through as you've read this book, such as how you've been able to unravel what happened to you, how your wounds are healing, and your plans for breaking the cycle.

You may also choose to offer a cleansing prayer for a fresh start.

WHAT IF YOU STILL CAN'T MOVE ON?

Reconciliation may be messy, take multiple attempts, be laborious and incremental, and suffer setbacks. You may do everything right, which takes great courage, only to be shot down or further abandoned. If after all your efforts you are still unable to rebuild your relationship, or if you still have unresolved issues after reading or discussing parts 1 and 2 of this book with a group, then you should seek professional Christian counseling.

It is a sign of strength to seek advice, and equally a sign of weakness *not* to. The single most important thing in selecting a counselor is "fit." There are many counseling styles and methods. Shop and ask around—like you would for a doctor who specializes in an area of medicine—to find a counselor who fits your needs and style.

You can also find an extensive list of Christian counselors at psychologytoday.com. You can search by location, type of therapy, specific issues, and more. You can also specify that you're looking for Christian counseling.

CONCLUSION

Here's the broken-boy dilemma: what happened to you is not your fault, but you're still responsible for what happens next.

In part 3, we will explore what you've been doing to yourself and others because of what was done to you—and how you can break the cycle going forward.

REFLECTION AND DISCUSSION

1. Have you attempted to have a crucial conversation with your parents about your childhood wounds? If so, how did it go? If not, what is keeping this conversation from happening?

2. Which next step suits your situation best—keep doing what you're doing, initiate a crucial conversation, have a facilitated session, or set boundaries? Why is this the next best step for you?

3. Obviously, there's a natural tension between the need for action and the desire to avoid a potential negative outcome. With that in mind, what is one thing you can do this week to overcome your reluctance and reach out to your parents?

PART 3

BREAKING THE CYCLE

14

THE JOY OF WALKING
WITH A LIMP

FOR TWO YEARS I battled an autoimmune disease. At one point I was so weak, I couldn't pick up a coffee mug or squeeze a honey bottle.

Every time the doctor asked me, "How would you describe your pain on a scale of 1 to 10?" I answered, "About a 4."

But pain is subjective, right? So I printed a pain assessment chart and took it to one of my appointments. When my doctor asked, "And how would you describe your pain today?" I whipped out the chart.

"I've been telling you my pain is a 4," I said, "but my 'chart face' says I'm really a 6 or 7."

As you can see from the Wong-Baker FACES Pain Rating Scale, I was in *severe* pain, but the doctor was hearing (and treating me for) *moderate* pain.

Wong-Baker FACES® Pain Rating Scale

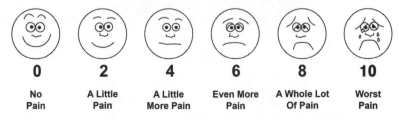

0	2	4	6	8	10
No Pain	A Little Pain	A Little More Pain	Even More Pain	A Whole Lot Of Pain	Worst Pain

©1983 Wong-Baker FACES Foundation. www.WongBakerFACES.org Used with permission.
Originally published in *Whaley & Wong's Nursing Care of Infants and Children*. ©Elsevier Inc. Wording modified for adult use.

Until I had the pain assessment chart as a reference point, I didn't understand how to evaluate my physical pain. Likewise, without a reference point, we won't understand how to evaluate our childhood pain.

While the Wong-Baker scale is intended only for physical pain, a similar scale could help us to think through childhood wounds. Before counseling, if someone had asked me to describe how I felt, I would have said, "I'm a 4." But if I had looked at a faces chart, I would have recognized that the leftover pain from my childhood wounds was never less than a 6, and sometimes 8 or more.

Today, my childhood wounds have mostly healed, and I can gratefully report that I'm usually only a 2 on the pain chart. That said, I still have residual symptoms that make me vulnerable to flare-ups. Sometimes I spike to a 4 to 6, or worse.

"Residual symptoms that flare up" is a good way to understand what's left over *after* we heal from childhood wounds.

All of us who have ever been broken boys will have flare-ups because, to some degree, we all live with the residual pain of what happened to us. We all have an emotional limp.

WALKING WITH A LIMP

A limp is a good metaphor for what's left over after healing takes place. As a badly crushed leg will heal but leave a physical limp, so a badly crushed soul will heal but leave an emotional limp.

Our limp is the residual effect our childhood wounds have on everyday encounters—our tendency to overreact to people and situations that remind us of our old wounds.

In the past, your overreaction happened at a subconscious level. You were easily offended. You lashed out. You sulked and withdrew. You damaged your relationships. But you didn't know why.

No one wants to walk around angry, sad, anxious, impatient, mean, unfaithful, snarky, or out of control. Yet that's exactly what happens when we don't know how to walk with our limp.

But knowledge is power. Now that you understand what happened to you and have started the healing process, you can take control. You can successfully—joyfully—live with your limp. Even if it's for the rest of your life.

RESIDUAL SYMPTOMS

Currently, what are the symptoms of your limp? Do you still get angry too quickly? Do you have inexplicable mood swings? Do you still get disproportionately upset when you're not treated with respect? When people lie? When people let you down? Do you have an exaggerated need to be loved, appear successful, or feel important?

Do you still have a hard time controlling your emotions when you want to discuss something that you don't think is right? Are you still guessing at healthy male behavior? Do you take out your pain on the people you love such as your wife, children, family, friends, or colleagues?

The most clear-cut symptom of my limp, for example, is that I still tend to see everything through the lens of abandonment. Every day I'm tempted to think people don't really care about me—even though I know that's a lie straight from the lips of the devil. It's #1 on the master list of nine characteristics shared by broken boys.

I dread that gut punch of being abandoned again. My lowest moments have always been when I've felt excluded, left behind, or taken for granted, or when my opinions no longer matter. As soon as I have a thought like *They don't want me anymore*, all the wind leaves my sails. Then I'm tempted to convince myself that I don't want them either.

Abandonment is part of my story. And the residual effects of that reality render me susceptible to flare-ups. It's part of my limp.

By God's grace and the power of the Holy Spirit, I rarely act on that temptation. But when I forget to put on my spiritual glasses to correct for abandonment, that's the first thing I see.

The second most pronounced symptom of my limp? It's characteristic #2—I'm oversensitive and often misread what people intend. There's a pervasive sense that I'm not good enough to deserve their love. It's a leftover insecurity—the third most prominent symptom of my limp (characteristic #5 on our master list). That's one reason I appreciate reassurance so much.

My limp explains why I've kept my inner circle small. All my best friends have been men who unconditionally loved and respected me. I never felt they were judging me or would betray or desert me, even if we had the occasional conflict. I never doubted that they cared about me as much as I cared about them.

Some people might say I'm damaged goods. Some might say you are too. I would reply like the apostle Paul, who shared this experience about his own limp:

> Three times I pleaded with the Lord to take it away
> from me. But he said to me, "My grace is sufficient
> for you, for my power is made perfect in weakness."
> Therefore I will boast all the more gladly about my
> weaknesses, so that Christ's power may rest on me.
> That is why, for Christ's sake, I delight in weaknesses,
> in insults, in hardships, in persecutions, in difficulties.
> For when I am weak, then I am strong.
>
> 2 CORINTHIANS 12:8-10

I hope you eventually make a full recovery. I pray that God will mend every trace of brokenness. But if you plead and God doesn't mend you completely, may this passage be your constant companion, as it is for me.

EVALUATING YOUR LIMP

If you badly crushed your leg and make an appointment for physical therapy after it heals, the first thing your therapist will do is evaluate where you are today. Then they will ask, "What are your goals? What percentage of motion do you want to recover?"

That's a good approach for creating an accurate picture of your emotional limp today and where you want to end up.

In the space provided, record the "emotional pain" from your childhood wounds—(1) when you started this book, (2) how you feel today, and (3) where you hope to end up in five years for each of the nine characteristics. While the Wong-Baker chart is for physical pain only, you may find it helpful to refer back to the chart on page 168.

For example:

	WHEN YOU STARTED	TODAY	IN FIVE YEARS
You have a hard time believing people really care about you.	7	5	2

Now consider your past and current pain levels, as well as your goals for recovery:

9 CHARACTERISTICS	WHEN YOU STARTED	TODAY	IN FIVE YEARS
1. You have a hard time believing people really care about you.			
2. You are oversensitive and often misread what people intend.			
3. You are easily angered.			
4. You're not sure what healthy male behavior looks like.			
5. You're insecure and need constant reassurance.			
6. You have dramatic mood swings and don't know why.			

9 CHARACTERISTICS	WHEN YOU STARTED	TODAY	IN FIVE YEARS
7. You're either "the responsible son" or especially immature for your age.			
8. You can't get rid of the negative voices in your head.			
9. You've cut yourself off from family members emotionally or physically.			

What did you learn about the severity of your childhood wounds from this exercise? Take a moment to acknowledge and celebrate the progress you've made so far. Where are you still vulnerable to flare-ups that make you limp?

Let's explore the biblical process for turning your limp into joy.

GOD'S LARGER PURPOSE

I heard a story about a group of women reading a passage in Malachi 3:2, in which Jesus is foretold as "a refiner's fire." To satisfy her curiosity, one of the women made an appointment with a silversmith to watch him work.

He took the raw silver and placed it onto the hottest part of the fire, explaining that this was essential to burn off the impurities.

She watched for a while and then asked, "Do you have to sit here the whole time?"

"Oh yes," he said. "I have to stay here the whole time because if I don't, and the refining process goes too far, it will destroy the silver." She was reminded of Malachi 3:3, which says, "He will sit as a refiner and purifier of silver."

After watching a while longer, she asked, "How do you know when the silver has been properly refined?"

"Ah, that's simple," he said. "When I can see my reflection in the silver, I know my work is complete."

James 1:2-4 says,

Consider it pure joy, my brothers and sisters, whenever you face trials of many kinds, because you know that the testing of your faith produces perseverance. Let perseverance finish its work so that you may be mature and complete, not lacking anything.

The "it" refers to your *circumstances*—including the people and situations that trigger one of the nine characteristics to rear its ugly head.

The "trials of many kinds" are your residual symptoms that flare up.

The "testing of your faith" is how God works in your flare-ups to refine you.

You and I can handle almost any amount of testing if we think it's for a greater purpose. There is comfort *in* testing because there is purpose *to* testing. The purpose of testing is to produce the "perseverance" that helps us become "mature and complete, not lacking anything"—like finished silver that reflects Jesus' image.

For that reason, James says we should consider our circumstances "pure joy." His advice aligns with that of Jesus, Peter, and Paul.[1]

Your joy doesn't have to depend on your circumstances.

Rather, joy is the attitude of the man who understands the larger purpose of what God is doing in his circumstances.

WHAT IF GOD NEVER REMOVES YOUR LIMP?

Kintsugi is a Japanese art of repairing broken pottery that uses gold to repair the cracks. By drawing attention to imperfections instead of concealing them, kintsugi artisans create something that is not only stronger than it was but has more character and beauty.

Rather than trying to conceal your limp, acknowledge it. There's joy in accepting that a limp is normal—even beautiful.

Dysfunction is so common that it need not be a scarlet letter of shame or a stigma. Rather, personal vulnerability—allowing other people to see your limp—gives others a reason to identify with and relate to you on a more personal level.

Once the apostle Paul accepted God was not going to take away his limp, he pivoted and said, "Therefore I will boast all the more gladly about my weaknesses, so that Christ's power may rest on me" (2 Corinthians 12:9). Accepting that you may have a limp that won't go away completely will give you power over it.

Understanding your limp is foundational to breaking the cycle. Equally foundational is owning how you have weaponized your old wounds. We'll take that up after the reflection and discussion questions.

REFLECTION AND DISCUSSION

1. How much emotional pain are you in right now? How does that compare to when you started?

2. How would you describe your limp? Refer to your assessment on pages 172-173.

3. How might you respond if your limp never goes away? Use Paul's response in 2 Corinthians 12:8-10 as a template for your answer.

4. A key idea for this chapter is "Joy is the attitude of the man who understands the larger purpose of what God is doing in his circumstances." Do you, or can you, choose joy in the face of pain—even if you must limp for the rest of your life?

15

OWNING THE WAYS YOU'VE WEAPONIZED YOUR WOUNDS

WHEN I QUIT HIGH SCHOOL, my dad drove me to the Army enlistment center. He was having headaches and planned to get the prescription for his glasses checked. Once I was gone, however, his headaches stopped.

So far, we've focused on the damage done to us. Now we come to the damage *we've* caused.

I weaponized my childhood wounds by acting out against my father, mother, brothers, wife, and children. For example, a small perceived slight would reinforce the "nobody cares about me" narrative, and I would lash out with angry words or pout, or both. I didn't mean to, but it happened. Maybe you did—or are doing—the same.

To authentically break the cycle, we must own all the ways

in which we have weaponized our childhood wounds and seek forgiveness.

The focus in this stage of healing is to confess if you have retaliated or escalated what happened to you, apologize, make amends, and ask for forgiveness.

That said, it's worth mentioning again: under no circumstances are you in any way responsible to apologize or seek forgiveness for abusive behavior against you, whether physical, emotional, or sexual, even if someone tries to blame you in some way or manipulate you into thinking it was your fault.

Rather, the purpose of this chapter is twofold: (1) to lead us into humility, godly sorrow, and repentance for how we may have hurt others—often in the same ways we were hurt, thus repeating the cycle; and (2) to provide a template for action that we can adapt for our needs.

INITIATING CHANGE

In this book, I always take your side and want the best for you. Along those lines, for you to go to the next level in healing your wounds—to authentically break the cycle—you must admit your mistakes, your errors in judgment, and your own sins. Once you do, it's like the moment of ignition on a rocket launch. The apostle John writes,

> If we claim to be without sin, we deceive ourselves and the truth is not in us. If we confess our sins, he is faithful and just and will forgive us our sins and purify us from all unrighteousness.
>
> I JOHN 1:8-9

The most famous leader from the Second Great Awakening, Charles Finney, said, "It is of great importance that the sinner should be made to feel his guilt, and not left to the impression that he is unfortunate."[1]

Likewise, the apostle Paul understood you can't move forward until you feel the full gravity of your own sinfulness. Still, it made him sad to confront the people for whom he cared so much. He wrote,

> Even if I caused you sorrow by my letter, I do not regret it. Though I did regret it—I see that my letter hurt you, but only for a little while—yet now I am happy, not because you were made sorry, but because your sorrow led you to repentance. For you became sorrowful as God intended and so were not harmed in any way by us. Godly sorrow brings repentance that leads to salvation and leaves no regret, but worldly sorrow brings death. See what this godly sorrow has produced in you: what earnestness, what eagerness to clear yourselves, what indignation, what alarm, what longing, what concern, what readiness to see justice done. At every point you have proved yourselves to be innocent in this matter.
>
> 2 CORINTHIANS 7:8-11

I care for you in much the same way. My purpose in this chapter is not to dig up painful memories or to accuse or shame you. Rather, it's to lead you to life and growth.

Repentance, for our purposes, means taking full ownership for the ways in which we have weaponized our childhood wounds. We do this by acknowledging our own sin, accepting full responsibility for it, saying "I'm sorry," explaining why we feel the need to apologize, asking for forgiveness, and earnestly committing to change our ways.

But how do we do this, exactly? Let's continue to burrow down until we have a clear picture of the steps each of us needs to take.

OWNING WHAT YOU'VE DONE

As previously stated, nearly every effective recovery program addresses the needs of the soul. However, much of their success also depends on another critical component: owning one's mistakes.

Take a closer look at steps 4 through 10 from Alcoholics Anonymous, because they paint a near-perfect picture of how you can own your mistakes and sins:

4. Made a searching and fearless moral inventory of ourselves.
5. Admitted to God, to ourselves, and to another human being the exact nature of our wrongs.
6. Were entirely ready to have God remove all these defects of character.
7. Humbly asked Him to remove our shortcomings.
8. Made a list of all persons we had harmed, and became willing to make amends to them all.
9. Made direct amends to such people wherever possible, except when to do so would injure them or others.

10. Continued to take personal inventory and when we were wrong promptly admitted it.[2]

Here's a guide you can use, adapted from those steps, for breaking the cycle in your own life. (In the Reflection and Discussion section, you will have an opportunity to work through these steps.)

1. Make a searching and fearless moral inventory of yourself.
2. Admit to God, yourself, and another person the exact nature of your sins.
3. Be ready for God to remove all your defects.
4. Humbly ask God to take away any of the nine characteristics that describe you.
5. Make a list of everyone you've wounded and make amends to each person, if possible.
6. Continue assessing yourself and be quick to confess when you're wrong.

OWNING MY MISTAKES: AN EXAMPLE

Once when I was preparing to teach a Bible study on anger, I read, "Do not be quickly provoked in your spirit, for anger resides in the lap of fools" (Ecclesiastes 7:9).

Everyone gets angry. But to be "quickly provoked in your spirit" is more. It's characteristic #3: "You are easily angered."

After reading that verse, I felt compelled to write a letter to our adult children in which I owned my anger. With their permission, I include the unedited version here to give you an example of what it looked like when I reflected, owned my mistakes, and took full responsibility:[3]

Jen and John,

It has been an interesting journey since my dad and mom died. When my mother passed, I didn't really miss her, and thought that was pretty odd. So, as you know, I got some counseling that was very helpful. But, as with all such matters of the heart and worldview, it's a long-term process.

I am reteaching The Man in the Mirror *in a "remix." Yesterday I spoke on anger. Over the last several weeks I have been reading several books and thinking about the topic.*

The bottom line is that for the first time I locked in on a category that I've been calling "an angry spirit."

I told my men how there are two places an angry spirit tends to come out: home and work. But at work, the consequences are so catastrophic to employment, identity, etc. that a man forces himself to be under control. Indeed, I never once lost my temper at the office. Instead, as I told my men, I stuffed it and brought it home.

I also taught my men that, generally, men who were fathered well are not angry, and men who were not fathered well are angry. Obviously generalizations, but generally true. The resulting anger is "free-floating." In other words, the man is angry but really doesn't know why. In fact, as in my case, he may simply deny he has an angry spirit.

I have several reasons for writing you today. First is to tell you that I am completely out of denial. On Friday I confessed to my men that I have had "an angry spirit" for most of my life. I am grateful to God that this seems to have gone away over the last few years.

Second is to tell you that I have had to grieve what could have been—both with my dad and how much better I could have been with you and your mother. Third is to tell you that I have repented to God with godly sorrow according to 2 Corinthians 7:11.

The final reason for writing is to apologize to you. Over the last few weeks, especially, God has brought to mind many if not most of the times I have exploded and lost my temper inappropriately with each of you. It has been painful, yet it has also changed my story about myself.

Denial is a much stronger force than I understood. But I am not in denial anymore. Frankly, it's embarrassing to confess this to you because all my life I wanted to be the perfect father and now I realize that I was not. It was the thing I most wanted to do with my life. I ask you to please forgive me. I want to forgive myself, but I'm finding that hard because I haven't brought this to you.

I love you very much and have always wanted and worked for your well-being. But now I realize that to give you complete peace I must accept responsibility for having an angry spirit when you were growing up.

If someone should read this letter, they wouldn't hear about all the great times, but that is not my purpose today. I have already worked through this with your mother.

Today, I am asking you to forgive me for the ways my angry spirit has hurt you, and I release you to God in prayer for whatever healing may be necessary in your heart.

Also, I realize you may have some things you want or need to say and/or ask me before offering me forgiveness. I would welcome the opportunity to hear from you about this. I will do anything for you.

I love you with all my heart,
Dad

Both of our children were gracious beyond words in their letters back to me. My heart was filled with peace after confessing and asking for their forgiveness.

This excerpt from our daughter's letter reveals the crux of the process: "God is so good and faithful to break through our denials and defenses, painful as it is."

Will you allow God to work in your heart and guide you through a similar process in your own life? It's *never* too late to try. The hard part is humbling yourself. Once you've done that, the rest is easy by comparison.

REFLECTION AND DISCUSSION

1. Who are the people you need to ask for forgiveness?

2. Using the following "6 Steps of Responsibility" as a template for action, write out your plan to own how you've weaponized your childhood wounds.

6 STEPS OF RESPONSIBILITY	SAMPLE PLAN	MY PLAN
1. Make a searching and fearless moral inventory of yourself.	I will write a self-searching letter to my wife and children.	
2. Admit to God, yourself, and another person the exact nature of your sins.	I will tell my book discussion group what I've done.	
3. Be ready for God to remove all your defects.	I will accept God's discipline as that of a father loving his son.	
4. Humbly ask God to take away any of the nine characteristics that describe you.	I will ask God for strength to change the nine characteristics.	

6 STEPS OF RESPONSIBILITY	SAMPLE PLAN	MY PLAN
5. Make a list of everyone you've wounded and make amends to each, if possible.	I will make a written list of everyone I've hurt and ask their forgiveness.	
6. Continue assessing yourself and be quick to confess when you're wrong.	I will continue in a small group that holds each other accountable.	

3. For the people you identified in step 5 above, which would be better: writing them a letter or sitting down with them face-to-face? Give yourself a deadline and stick to it. I promise you, it will be one of the most liberating and healing steps you ever take. And if the people you want to apologize to, such as a parent or child, are deceased or unwilling to respond, you still have options. Consider writing out what you want to say and then sharing it with your spouse, a close friend, or your small group. You can also visit a meaningful place, such as a church or cemetery, to say what you need to say.

CHANGING THE TRAJECTORY OF YOUR MARRIAGE

WHILE WE WERE DATING, my wife said, "When we first met, I was surprised at how your father allowed you four boys to talk so disrespectfully to your mother. My dad would never let that happen." She recalls that I stopped once she brought it to my attention.

Based on the experiences I had growing up, I came into marriage with a hodgepodge of distorted views about how to be a good husband. You probably did too. Childhood memories can warp our picture of what a good husband looks like.

THE PROBLEM

The number one place where flare-ups from your childhood wounds will appear is your marriage.

Do any of these sound familiar?

- You're still overreacting (or underreacting) to your wife.
- You're prickly when she suggests you might be wrong.
- You pout when she doesn't give you enough attention because she's worn out from taking care of the kids.
- You get angry or insecure (or both) when she doesn't speak your love language as often as you wish she would.

If you're going to have a flare-up, where do you think it will happen? At work? Not likely. The stakes are too high. You'll be held in check by the potential loss of reputation, the chance of sabotaging your opportunities for advancement, or even the possibility of losing your job.

Instead, we tend to stuff our feelings and bring them home. Then some small issue sets us off because we were already exasperated. To make matters worse, we blow the perceived offense completely out of proportion because of residual pain from our childhood wounds.

WHAT'S GOING ON?

If you struggle with a still-open wound or have a flare-up, doesn't it make perfect sense that your most personal, frequent, and intense relationships would be the most vulnerable?

Marriage is the most intimate human relationship possible, and there isn't a close second. Marriage can be the safest, most comfortable relationship of all—that place where no matter what happened today, you know your wife will love and accept you as you are. It is simultaneously the most intense and the most potentially volatile of all possible relationships.

If your marriage is suffering because of too many flare-ups from lingering childhood wounds, this chapter will help you understand what's happening, why, and what you can do about it. I'm going to show you how to respond with maturity, and especially spiritual maturity. You won't get it right *every* time, but you can get better *over* time.

DOING TO HER WHAT WAS DONE TO YOU

If you're married, can you picture your wife making any of these statements to describe you?

- "My husband is oversensitive; I walk on eggshells."
- "He has dramatic mood swings."
- "He is obsessively driven and has little time for me."
- "He is immature and doesn't take responsibility for things."
- "He is negative."
- "He is unforgiving and holds grudges."
- "He takes out his frustrations on me."

Here's the core issue: if you have unhealed wounds, you are at risk of repeating the cycle (whether partially or in full). Just as you thought your parents were passive, absent, permissive, enabling, angry, demanding, or belittling, your wife may think the same of you, with varying degrees of intensity.

The good news is this isn't a lifetime sentence. As you are

healing, the cracks in your marriage will be healed too. Let me show you how to do something heroic for your marriage.

CORRECTED VISION FOR YOUR MARRIAGE

When an optometrist fits you for glasses, the goal is to correct any distortions to your vision. Like a pair of spiritual glasses, the biblical process for healing childhood wounds will correct the distorted views you may have about marriage. How clear is your vision for marriage and for your role as a husband?

The apostle Paul paints a clear picture of how husbands and wives can have a healthy, happy marriage. Central to it is the idea of *mutual submission*, described in his letter to the Ephesians.

Verses 21 and 33 of chapter 5 bookend the passage with an admonition to practice mutual love, respect, and submission. The first bookend, verse 21, says, "Submit to one another out of reverence for Christ."

Verse 33, the other bookend, concludes with the kind of mutual submission we need from each other: "Each one of you also must love his wife as he loves himself, and the wife must respect her husband."

For you, mutual submission means that you feel respected by your wife. For her, mutual submission means that she feels you love her as much as you love yourself.

Paul addresses husbands directly in verses 5:25-32 to elaborate on what this looks like:

> Husbands, love your wives, just as Christ loved the
> church and gave himself up for her to make her holy,
> cleansing her by the washing with water through the

word, and to present her to himself as a radiant church, without stain or wrinkle or any other blemish, but holy and blameless. In this same way, husbands ought to love their wives as their own bodies. He who loves his wife loves himself. After all, no one ever hated their own body, but they feed and care for their body, just as Christ does the church—for we are members of his body. "For this reason a man will leave his father and mother and be united to his wife, and the two will become one flesh." This is a profound mystery—but I am talking about Christ and the church.

He gives a big call to action to married men: "Husbands, love your wives, just as Christ loved the church *and gave himself up for her.*" Right out of the gate, Paul is saying that the biblical prescription for correcting distortions in your vision for marriage is sacrificial love.

But beyond sacrifice, how did Christ love the church? What is the model that we are supposed to imitate on a practical, day-to-day level?

"Christ" is a title of Jesus that refers to his roles as prophet, priest, and king for his church. I've written extensively about this passage elsewhere, but let me summarize how you can strive to love your wife in this way, based on Paul's guidance.

The Role of a Prophet

At the heart of the life of a prophet is a commitment to listen to God and then share God's message with others.

You can help your wife grow in her faith by reading God's Word for yourself, sharing what you're learning with her, having spiritual conversations together, and leading your family in church participation and devotions.

If you don't yet have time in your daily routine to spend with God, that's your first step in loving your wife as a prophet would.

The Role of a Priest

In the Old Testament, a priest would mediate between God and the people. Now, Jesus is our High Priest who mediates on our behalf (see Hebrews 4:14-16).

But you can still love your wife in the manner of a priest by nurturing her and praying for her. Spend time in prayer each day, bringing the needs and concerns of your wife before God. You may be the only person in the world praying for her on a regular basis.

The Role of a King

Jesus, referred to as the King of kings, lived as a humble servant. With that model in mind, the role of a king is threefold: (1) to lead, (2) to provide, and (3) to protect.

You can love your wife as a king would by leading her—by example—toward Christ and not away from him.

Providing for her as a king means working diligently to provide stability—to meet her physical needs financially, yes, but also to meet her emotional needs.

Protecting her involves keeping her safe from physical danger, certainly. But you are also called to protect her from spiritual and emotional danger, and this includes protecting yourself from temptations that, if acted upon, might hinder your relationship with your wife.

With Jesus as your model, your attitude should be "I need to be a great king because my wife needs to be treated like a great queen."

RECASTING THE VISION FOR YOUR MARRIAGE

It's 3:00 a.m. You wake up and start going over in your mind what happened yesterday with your wife. By the time she gets up, you're walking around with bruised feelings and a chip on your shoulder. What can you do to get yourself under control before you say or do something stupid?

Here are a few practical, cycle-breaking steps you can take to recast the way you think about your wife—not only during moments like these but also before they strike.

Increase Your Self-Awareness

Here's the problem with quickly assuming why your wife is behaving a certain way: your interpretation is just as likely to be wrong as right.

Human nature pushes us to attribute motives to the behavior and actions of another person, even if we don't know what they are. And the attribution is usually negative. Furthermore, what you think about unknown motives often reflects what *your* motives would be in the same situation.

Instead of rushing to assign a motive, take some time to cool off and think. A good rule of thumb is to keep quiet if you don't know—with certainty—what you're talking about. To paraphrase the humorist Sam Levenson, it's easy to be wise. Just think of something stupid and then don't say it.

Then, once you feel calmer, try to name the emotion you're

feeling, such as anger or self-pity. Does whatever emotion you've identified correspond to one of the nine characteristics?

When you have traced the emotion to a root cause, let that be an epiphany for you. Take advantage of your increased self-awareness to adjust the story you've been telling yourself about your wife.

Ask God for Help

As soon as you experience negative thoughts or an intense emotion in response to a trigger or conflict, pray. Ask God for wisdom, power, and strength to respond with maturity. Ask him to fill you with his Holy Spirit.

In fact, all the qualities you need to not over- or underreact are the fruit of being filled by God's Spirit:

> The fruit of the Spirit is love, joy, peace, forbearance [patience], kindness, goodness, faithfulness, gentleness and self-control.
>
> GALATIANS 5:22-23

In contrast, *not* asking God for help and letting your anger run its course can lead to catastrophe: "If you bite and devour each other, watch out or you will be destroyed by each other" (Galatians 5:15).

But when you battle, through prayer, the negative thoughts and emotions threatening to overwhelm you, God will give you the fruit of his Spirit so that you can make the right choices: "Walk by the Spirit, and you will not gratify the desires of the flesh [sinful nature]. For the flesh desires what is contrary to the

Spirit, and the Spirit what is contrary to the flesh" (Galatians 5:16-17).

Retrain Your Mind

If you are tired of feeling controlled by your childhood wounds and want to retrain your thoughts, heart, and responses, then commit to reading the Bible on a regular basis. I recommend five or more days a week—even if it's only two or three pages a day.

The Bible will open up your heart and mind to a fundamentally different way of seeing yourself, your wife, and the world:

> The word of God is alive and active. Sharper than any double-edged sword, it penetrates even to dividing soul and spirit, joints and marrow; it judges the thoughts and attitudes of the heart.
>
> HEBREWS 4:12

If you're not familiar with Bible reading, start with the Gospel of John in the New Testament. It has twenty-one short chapters, so you can read one chapter a day and finish it in less than a month.

Then continue reading other parts of the New Testament. For example, if you read five chapters per week, you can read all 260 chapters of the New Testament in a year. The impact on your life—including your marriage—will be powerful!

I'm also a big believer in the power of reading Christian literature. I don't believe in the power of Christian literature because I write books; rather, I write books because I believe in the power of Christian literature. I have repeatedly seen how a man will get hold of a book and then God will use the book to get hold of the man.

I'm sure that parts of this book have resonated with you more than others. Keep it nearby so you can reread those sections when you're tempted to act out of pain—especially if it's 3:00 a.m.

Add other books to your library that connect with you, including books about how to strengthen your marriage.

Make a List

Louis Agassiz said, "A pencil is one of the best of eyes."[1] Writing can provide you with a perspective and objectivity that can otherwise be difficult to obtain.

You have done some writing during this process already, such as "The Truth I Need to Face" on pages 85-86 in chapter 7. Why not keep it going and add to it?

Start a journal by writing out any thoughts and feelings related to your childhood wounds in general—and how they affect your marriage in particular. Don't overthink it; your journal is for your use only.

Here is a simple writing prompt to get started. Thinking about your wife, make a list of her strengths and anything you admire or appreciate about her. A friend once said, "We're down on what we're not up on." With that in mind, being—and staying—up on the positives keeps us from spiraling when we face challenges. For example:

- She is kind to strangers.
- We have the same sense of humor.
- She is a great mother.

- She is a faithful friend to our neighbors.
- She has a strong work ethic.
- She always says "Thank you" when I hold the door for her.
- She tells the truth, even when it hurts, but she's gracious about it.

What's on your list? Let those thoughts be the narrative you play over and over in your mind.

After you have written down all the positives, only then should you write down what's bothering you. For example, you might write that you are angry because you don't feel like your wife really cares about you. You may find that your frustrations and negative feelings look different to you (a) in writing, and (b) in context of the positives.

CONCLUSION

Because of your childhood wounds, you've been one way for decades, so be patient and give the changes you're making time to become a part of you.

Above all, if you will let God correct your vision in whatever ways are needed and allow these biblical principles to permeate your heart, you will change the trajectory of your marriage. You will eventually stop most of the over- and underreactions you've been directing at your wife.

REFLECTION AND DISCUSSION

1. If married, what is the wound or flare-up that routinely sabotages your marriage?

2. What is something you want to begin doing to love your wife as Christ loved the church, using the three roles (prophet, priest, king) described in this chapter?

3. "I need to be a great king because my wife needs to be treated like a great queen." If you want that idea to be your attitude, start by making a list of your wife's strengths and what you admire and appreciate about her. Use a journal or the space below:

PARENTING YOUR OWN CHILDREN

WHEN PATSY AND I brought our first child home from the hospital, all three of us were exhausted. I lay down and cradled our new daughter on my chest. The warmth of that tiny body—a living person I helped create—and the thump, thump, thump of her acorn-sized heart will always be a top-ten memory for me.

If you're like me, nothing is more important than giving your children what you missed. But that thumping heartbeat shocked me back to the reality that *I had no idea how to be a parent.*

Because you grew up dysfunctional, like me, you've had to guess at normal male behavior—and that includes how to be a great dad. In this chapter, you're going to see God's master plan for how to be that great dad who makes a difference.

The plan is a concept called *fathering the heart*, and it has power to break the cycle of intergenerational neglect or abuse. Fathering your child's heart is how you can give them the right cocktail of love, structure, roots, and wings.

FATHERING THE HEART VERSUS FATHERING FOR PERFORMANCE

Fathering for *performance* is the opposite of fathering the *heart*. Fathering for performance neglects love and structure, focusing instead on trying to get children to behave properly. The parenting goals for someone who is fathering for performance include making sure his children

- know their place—and stay in it,
- show him respect,
- get good grades so they can make their dad proud,
- don't embarrass him in public by acting like children, and
- stay off his bad side.

Children fathered this way think, *All my dad wants is for me to keep my mouth shut, obey his rules, and meet his expectations. But I never measure up.* Or *My dad never does anything with me. He doesn't show me how to do things. He's not interested in me at all.*

The man fathering for performance is consumed with asking, *What is my child doing? How can I get them to behave?*

But the man who is aiming to father the heart asks, *Why is my child behaving like this? How can I mentor them to change the attitude of their heart?*

Here is a side-by-side comparison:[1]

FATHERING FOR PERFORMANCE	FATHERING THE HEART
Emphasizes conformity	Emphasizes transformation
Creates an atmosphere of fear	Creates an atmosphere of safety
Prioritizes parental control	Allows freedom within boundaries
Focuses on present performance	Focuses on future development
Values playing a role	Values authenticity
Comes down hard on children	Comes alongside children
Interacts on the surface	Fosters true communication
Assumes the worst	Believes the best
Protects the status quo	Prioritizes growth and change
Offers pronouncements from on high	Encourages questions and discussion
Uses people, fostering a "business relationship"	Makes space for intimacy and vulnerability

As you read over this chart, which of the two columns best describes your parenting approach? Give it some honest reflection. Regardless of where you're starting from, my hope is that this chapter will guide you in nurturing your children's hearts and helping them thrive.

Here are some practical ideas to help you live as a daily dad who's in the picture, regularly and liberally dispensing doses of love, structure, roots, and wings.

LOVE

Love takes many forms, but it should always include verbal expression when it comes to your family. Never assume your children know you love them, believe in them, and are proud of them. In my childhood home, it went unsaid, and the damage was devastating.

Instead, consistently encourage your children with words. Try to tell each child "I love you" and "I'm proud of you" at least once every day. Sound like too much? It's not. Try it and see.

Love looks like conversation. It's never a good idea to say, "I'm too busy" when a child wants to talk. If you can't talk then, tell them when you can talk later. Make sure you take time to discern what your child needs in each situation—whether words of comfort and solace, of encouragement and inspiration, or of admonition. Sometimes they might need a hug, but sometimes they might need a kick in the pants. Love tries to make the right call.

Love also expresses itself in nonverbal ways. Never underestimate the healing power of physical touch. Hug your kids every day. (If they are grown and out of the house, embrace them when you see them.) If you don't regularly show your children love through physical affection, they will likely look for physical affection elsewhere, prematurely. A missed hug is gone forever.

Love also requires time. The best way to spend time with your kids is the way in which *they* want to spend it. If they like drones, go to a drone park. If they like cheerleading, go to their games. If they like karate, learn karate with them.

Schedule a recurring appointment with your kids. For example, every Tuesday I alternated taking one of our two children to dinner, followed by an activity such as going to a movie, racing go-karts, playing games at the arcade, or eating ice cream.

Another way you can invest time is to involve your children in planning a family vacation. Some of my fondest and most vivid childhood memories revolve around family vacations.

In chapter 3, you completed reflection exercises to describe how you felt your parents did at giving you love, structure, roots, and wings. Now I want you to flip the script and describe how you feel about what *you* are passing on to *your* kids.

REFLECTION EXERCISE:
In general, do you think you have loved your children the way they need to be loved?

| never | rarely | sometimes | usually | always |

STRUCTURE

Once our family hiked up Whiteside Mountain in North Carolina. We let our elementary-aged children walk along the edge of a cliff that plummets 750 feet to the canyon floor. We could do that because there were guardrails along the edge. The guardrails provided the structure our kids (and my wife and I!) needed to walk with confidence.

It's the same way with providing the right amount of structure for your children. Knowing your everyday rules, boundaries, and what to expect creates confidence, freedom, and a sense of security. When you build dependable guardrails, you father their hearts.

It allows you to break the cycle by steering clear of two problems. The first problem is *too much structure*.

Dysfunctional families are often "because I said so" homes. Parents are hyperfocused on behavior, getting children to conform and obey, and performance. Because love is not the primary governing principle, children are often insecure, filled with fears, and forced to play a role. Little or no attention is given to what's going on inside the child's heart, and because they are ruled with an iron hand, they flounder.

The second problem? *Not enough structure*.

King David—a great man and human ancestor of Jesus—was also the father of an incredibly flawed family. We find two clues in Scripture as to why David's family was so dysfunctional.

The first is a comment about his son Adonijah's misbehavior: "His father had never rebuked him by asking, 'Why do you behave as you do?'" (1 Kings 1:6). In other words, David was passive and permissive.

Then, 1 Chronicles 27:32 tells us that "Jehiel son of Hakmoni took care of the king's sons." Or, said another way, David was absent and uninvolved. He didn't provide enough structure.

Because David was a failure as a dad, his children suffered immensely. His son Amnon raped David's daughter Tamar. His son Absalom then killed Amnon. His son Adonijah attempted a palace coup. And eventually Absalom also rebelled and overthrew his father.

The dysfunction and resulting heartache created by David's lack of structure is an extreme and sobering example. Let it be a cautionary tale: your children need structure and boundaries. Build guardrails so they will be wise and confident about what's in- and out-of-bounds.

REFLECTION EXERCISE:

In general, do you think you have provided your children with the right amount of structure?

never	rarely	sometimes	usually	always

ROOTS

Giving your children roots requires you to satisfy a broad spectrum of needs for raising healthy, secure, self-confident children. Dozens of theories and thousands of books address this, but one way to simplify what children need is captured in a model often used by psychologists called Maslow's Hierarchy of Needs.[2]

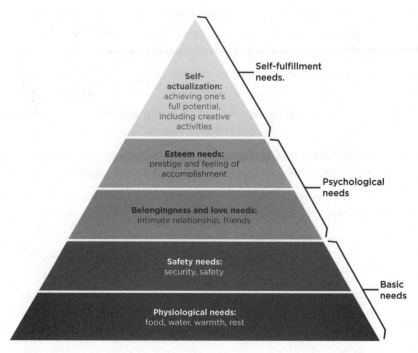

The model posits that the needs at the bottom of the hierarchy (like food, shelter, and safety) must be satisfied before someone has the ability and freedom to focus on the higher-level needs (like self-esteem or reaching their full potential).

As you can see, your children's needs range from very basic to profound. Yes, providing roots means putting a roof over their heads and food on the table. But providing roots also means giving your children the security of a safe, predictable, and stable home environment.

It means creating a space where your children feel protected, accepted, and loved unconditionally. They can count on you to give reasonable responses and to be predictable.

What a blessing it is, for example, that if your child faces bullies at school, he can still look forward to coming home to a stable environment. The best antidote to everything from peer pressure to insecurity is a caring, involved parent.

Since Maslow's hierarchy doesn't expressly include spiritual needs, you should add a category for "spiritual development" to your own list of the roots you want to nurture.

REFLECTION EXERCISE:
In general, do you think you have given your children roots?

never	rarely	sometimes	usually	always

WINGS

Nothing looms larger for you than to help each of your children develop their sense of identity—a clear conviction about who they are and what their lives are all about.

Of course, you will do some of this naturally from the day they're born. But the more intentional you are in fostering identity and independence now, the stronger their wings will be when they eventually leave the nest.

What are some of the ways in which you want to help your children to develop wings—to become mature, independent adults? To jump-start your thinking, jot down some answers to the following questions:

What are the competencies you want your children to acquire?

_____

_____

_____

_____

What beliefs, attitudes, and values do you hope they adopt?

_____

_____

_____

_____

What character traits do you hope they will develop?

_____

_____

_____

_____

_____

What key relationships would you like them to put in place?

_____

_____

_____

_____

Every child has natural aptitudes, abilities, and gifts. How can you encourage your children to develop theirs?

_____

_____

_____

_____

Once you have a clearer sense of the wings you want to give your children, share them around the dinner table. Do it in daily doses.

Another wing-strengthening activity is to have family devotions. Share your thoughts on a verse or topic, and then ask your children to share theirs. These conversations will help them build their sense of identity around who Christ says they are in him. The best routine for devotions is whatever works best for *your* family. When our kids were younger, we met three times a week before school for a fifteen-minute family devotion, and we took summers off. It was simple, and it worked.

As your children go through different ages and seasons, increasing their responsibilities will help bolster their self-confidence. An important wing-strengthener when they are starting out in school, for example, is teaching them how to study and complete assignments. As they continue to grow, you can help them explore their abilities and interests in various areas like athletics or the arts. All of these things will give their self-confidence a boost.

As they progress through adolescence, encouraging them to become more independent means helping them answer deeper questions about the meaning and purpose of life, how to know God, when and how to date, why sex is meant for the marriage relationship, what educational directions they can take after high school, what to look for in a spouse, and vocational options.

Whatever you decide to teach them is important, so be intentional about it.

REFLECTION EXERCISE:

In general, do you think you are giving your children wings?

| never | rarely | sometimes | usually | always |

ASKING GOD FOR HELP

At the end of the day, as parents, we are the ones most fully invested in giving our children love, structure, roots, and wings. Others may care deeply, but we are the ones God has ordained to watch over and nurture them. Building a healthy, happy home is a big responsibility—one that requires all the help we can get. At the top of the list is asking for God's help.

As the psalmist writes, "Unless the LORD builds the house, the builders labor in vain" (Psalm 127:1).

I hike and backpack solo. When people ask if I'm worried to go alone, I say, "I'm never really alone, because God is always with me. No matter what I encounter, together we are in the majority." Likewise, you and God are a majority in every situation. As such, be sure to ask for God's favor and wisdom through prayer along the way: "If any of you lacks wisdom, you should ask God, who gives generously to all without finding fault, and it will be given to you" (James 1:5).

If you aren't used to praying for your children and feel unsure of where to begin, consider making a list of hopes you have for their lives and character. For example, every day of my children's lives until they left home, these are the things I prayed for them to have:

- a saving faith
- a growing faith
- an independent faith
- a strong and healthy mind, body, and spirit
- a sense of purpose
- a desire for integrity
- a commitment to excellence
- an understanding of the ministry God has for them
- wisdom
- protection from drugs, alcohol, and premarital sex
- a desire to glorify the Lord in everything

In addition, I prayed that I would set aside quality time to spend with them, and I prayed for their future spouses.

Consider this: as your children's father, you (along with your wife) may be the only person in the world praying for them on a regular basis.

CONCLUSION

I left home because I didn't feel wanted. I didn't feel like anyone cared about me. That probably wasn't true, but that's the way I remember it—how I was made to feel.

But I will always wonder how our family could have been different if some older men had shown my dad how to father the hearts of his four sons. Just imagine how many other men there must be like my father—as well as their sons and daughters—left to wonder, *How did it all go so wrong?* It's a staggering thought, isn't it?

In the final chapter, I want to show you how you can pass along what you've learned and experienced to other men in our fraternal order of broken boys. Remember, there are millions of us.

REFLECTION AND DISCUSSION

1. How would you summarize the difference between fathering for performance and fathering the heart? (Refer to the table on page 205.)

2. Are you, or are you ready to be, a daily dad who's in the picture, liberally dispensing doses of love, structure, roots, and wings? What are the changes you've made, or need to make, for that to happen?

3. How did you rate yourself in the reflection exercises for
   love, structure, roots, and wings? Did you pick up any
   ideas that can be quickly and easily implemented?

HOW TO BE A FRIEND TO MEN WITH SIMILAR WOUNDS

YOU'VE MADE IT. Yes, you suffered greatly. You were weary and burdened. But now you're safely inside the fence—inside the wire. You've healed or, depending on the severity of your wounds, started to heal.

Yes, you walk with a limp. But you're hopeful and sense that you're going to be okay. Better than okay—you can feel that you're going to fulfill the Cycle Breaker's Credo (see page 81).

But there are still millions of other broken boys outside the wire. They live in a battle zone. They are still under fire. Still wounded.

These men are friends, neighbors, coworkers, sons, fathers, and brothers. They still carry around the leftover pain of their childhood wounds. They're still acting out. Withdrawing. Easily offended. Lashing out. They're still baffled by their behavior. They're still wondering, *Is this as good as it gets?*

Who will rescue these men?

WE ARE THE SOLUTION WE'VE BEEN LOOKING FOR

Do not be surprised if you find yourself drawn to help other men trying to break the cycle. The men most qualified to help other broken boys mend are the ones who have walked in their shoes.

The final step in Alcoholics Anonymous is "Having had a spiritual awakening as the result of these Steps, we tried to carry this message to alcoholics, and to practice these principles in all our affairs."[1]

While you're healing, you won't always have the capacity to care deeply about other men suffering from similar sorrows. That's understandable. But like a recovering alcoholic who helps other alcoholics, once you become a mended man, you can help other broken boys.

The healing you have received is not for you only. Through relationship, you can help those men understand what happened to them, heal their childhood wounds, and break the cycle.

Relationships are part of God's normal healing process. The apostle Paul said it like this:

Praise be to the God and Father of our Lord Jesus Christ, the Father of compassion and the God of all

comfort, who comforts us in all our troubles, so that
we can comfort those in any trouble with the comfort
we ourselves receive from God.

2 CORINTHIANS 1:3-4

You will find a deep sense of personal satisfaction and ful-
fillment by helping others with the help you yourself have
received.

In fact, every aspect of the biblical process of healing we've
been discussing works best when pursued in the context of
relationships. An eighty-five-year study by Harvard researchers
confirmed it: the number one key to a happy, healthy, and long
life is having positive relationships.[2]

Building relationships is the approach Jesus used. He gathered a small group of men around him and developed deep
relationships that changed them. Then they, in turn, built
relationships with others, who built relationships with others,
and it changed the world.

As you know firsthand, the nine characteristics make it difficult to form and sustain close friendships. Ironically, the more
desperately a man needs relationships, the harder it seems to be
for him to make them work.

As someone who understands and empathizes because
you've been there before, you can make a difference. When you
do, you'll find that helping another man change his life is one
of life's greatest joys.

Furthermore, when you're feeling down or stuck, serving
others is a great way to get out of a funk. The psychiatrist Karl
Menninger was asked what action he would recommend if a
person were to feel a nervous breakdown coming on. He said,

"Lock up your house, go across the railroad tracks, and find someone in need and do something for him."

If you're ready to get started, here are two easy entry points.

Get a Cup of Coffee

Start small and be intentional. Invite a man to get coffee with you. Most men will respond positively if they feel like you really care about them.

When you're together, the goal is to have a real conversation about real things. Once you've developed a rapport, ask the other man to share his story. You don't need a degree or special training to be helpful. The Kairos Prison Ministry has a slogan: "Listen, listen, love, love." That's it in a nutshell. Between the reflections and the exercises you've done while going through this book, you have more than enough knowledge to be a good listener.

After you've let him say everything he wants to say, offer to tell him your story. Ask permission; don't push. But since you heard him out, he will likely want to hear you out.

When you tell your story, be vulnerable and open. Share details about your life because that's what friends do. Like the apostle Paul, you can comfort him with the comfort you yourself have received from God.

After suffering with father wounds for much of his adult life—largely by himself—Craig experienced the power of sharing stories. He says,

> Being able to talk openly and process things with other guys—I'd never had that before. I began to realize that everything I was going through—my pain, and hurt,

and work addiction, and sin—these guys could relate.

It was powerful to suddenly find I wasn't the only one.

I wasn't alone anymore.

Start a Group

Invite a man or a few men to read this book with you and meet regularly to discuss the questions at the end of each chapter.

Set the tone for meetings through leading by example with vulnerability, empathy, and confidentiality. Make the group a safe place for men to talk about how the nine characteristics are affecting them and their marriages, children, jobs, and relationships with God.

Something powerful and synergistic happens when you're part of a group of men breaking the cycle together. Anthropologist Margaret Mead reportedly said, "Never doubt that a small group of thoughtful, committed citizens can change the world; indeed, it's the only thing that ever has."

For ideas and tips on starting a group, see the "Guide: How to Lead a Discussion Group" on page 231.

THE HIGH CALLING TO MEND BROKEN BOYS

Mending men is urgent work. The stakes are high—not only for men but for their families and communities. Building meaningful relationships with those men is key to helping them heal.

To see men experience the deepest and most lasting kind of healing and transformation, you can show them how to build the relationship that matters most—introduce them to Jesus.

A Chinese proverb says, "The best time to plant a tree was twenty years ago. The second-best time is now." Showing men how to become followers of Jesus now is what will make the most difference for them twenty years from now. Swiss psychiatrist Carl Jung observed,

> I have treated many hundreds of patients. . . . Among all my patients in the second half of life—that is to say, over thirty-five—there has not been one whose problem in the last resort was not that of finding a religious outlook on life. It is safe to say that every one of them fell ill because he had lost that which the living religions of every age have given their followers, and none of them has been really healed who did not regain his religious outlook.[3]

No matter how your friend, coworker, neighbor, or son got into his current situation—whether it's the wounds that hurt him or the pain he inflicts on others because of his wounds—the solution prescribed in our millennia-old process is to disciple him out. Making disciples through authentic relationships is God's designated way to release the power of his gospel on every problem men face.

Still not sure you're the man for the job? God works through the present and willing, not the absent and able. In the Bible, when the prophet Isaiah was healed, he heard the voice of the Lord saying, "Whom shall I send? And who will go for us?" Overwhelmed by what God had done for him, Isaiah was willing—even eager—to answer the call: "Here am I. Send me!" (Isaiah 6:8).

Will you go too? You may be just the man God can use to help other broken boys become mended men.

REFLECTION AND DISCUSSION

1. Do you feel far enough along in your healing to, as Paul said, "comfort those in any trouble with the comfort we ourselves receive from God"? Explain.

2. Who are the men around you who may be broken boys? If you're ready, which one of them could you invite for a cup of coffee over the next few days?

3. Who are the men you could invite to join you for a weekly discussion group? You would each read a chapter beforehand and then you would discuss the questions at the end of each chapter together. Make your group a safe place for men to talk about how the nine characteristics are affecting them and their marriages, children, places of work, and relationships with God. The "Guide: How to Lead a Discussion Group" at the end of this book has more ideas and best practices for using this book in a group.

4. Are there some men who helped you identify and heal your childhood wounds and break the cycle? Consider sending them a thank-you note.

AFTERWORD

THANK YOU FOR ALLOWING ME to be part of your story for a few hours. I genuinely hope and pray that God has used these pages to help you heal, or begin healing, from your childhood wounds and break the cycle for you and your family.

God loves you more than anyone can describe with mere words, and he only wants what's best for you. Like a loving father, he will provide everything you need to change your life. He has promised that over and over in the biblical process we've explored.

As your elder brother in the fraternal order of broken boys, I would like to leave you with four suggestions:

- First, reread the book. We've all rewatched a movie and said, "Okay, now I get it." The principle here is the same. You've been introduced to a lot of new terms and concepts. They will make a lot more sense on a second reading now that you can see the whole arc of the process.
- Second, be transparent with a friend or two. Almost all the meaningful change that I've observed in men's

lives has been, at least in part, because they engaged
in authentic relationships with other men. The key
is to be honest. And the magic is that instead of men
rejecting you, they will be drawn to your humility and
vulnerability.

- Third, discuss this book in a group. For you, of course.
But even if you don't need to discuss it, other men
do—especially younger men who are trying to figure out
what it means to be a healthy man, husband, and father
who is in the picture. You could make a real difference
in their lives. And if you don't help them, who will?

- Fourth, affirm or reaffirm your faith. My books cover a
full range of men's topics, but each was written to help
you overcome some specific obstacle to faith. In this
book, that obstacle is your lingering childhood wounds.
I sincerely hope you have experienced enough progress
that you feel compelled to affirm, reaffirm, or renew
your faith in Jesus.

We've probably never met, but I believe you can do this.
You can change your life with God's help and the right people.
Don't stop now. Let this book be the beginning of a beautiful
new season of life for you.

ACKNOWLEDGMENTS

TO CREATE AND PUBLISH THIS BOOK required the skill, wisdom, and connections of dozens of people with hundreds of years of collective experience. Like credits that roll at the end of a movie, some of their contributions have been so important that they must be publicly thanked.

First and foremost, my wife, Patsy, has always been my first reader and best sounding board. Our daughter, Jen, made key recommendations. Lottie Hillard is the counselor who first helped me understand that I could face the truth, confront my childhood wounds, and heal.

My other first readers are all men whose feedback identified where I needed to explain myself better if I was to pierce, rather than bounce off, the target. Thank you, Jeff Bach, Connor Jones, Aubrey Truex, Winn Truitt, and John Vonberg. Thank you also to Ruth Ford, who did the first substantive edit and helped take out the trash—as she has helped me do for thirty years.

I especially want to thank Jamie Turco for copy and substantive editing. No one helps me say what needs to be said, the way I like to write it, better than Jamie. Besides being a brilliant colleague for eighteen years—and she's still under forty!—she is my dear friend.

Erik and Robert Wolgemuth have been my friends and literary agents for more than thirty years. Their love for me personally, as well as their belief in my message, has allowed me to work with the finest publishers in the world of Christian literature. I'm profoundly grateful.

The backing of the team at Man in the Mirror—and their enthusiasm for this book in particular—has been a strong breeze in my sails every day. Thank you.

From the first day I met Jon Farrar at Tyndale House Publishers, I knew Tyndale would be a perfect match for the mission of this book. I was not wrong. Their zeal and passion to get this message into the hands of as many men as possible has been as humbling as it has been thrilling. I would especially like to mention and thank the following Tyndale team members: Stephanie Abrassart, Ron Beers, Donna Berg, Wendie Connors, Lois Davisson, Kaylee Frank, Cassidy Gage, Alan Huizenga, Claire Lloyd, Andrea Martin, Jennifer Phelps, Dean Renninger, and Jonathan Schindler. And thanks to Sarah Adams and Jeremy Park for their work on the audiobook.

GUIDE: HOW TO LEAD
A DISCUSSION GROUP

You don't have to be an experienced teacher or discussion leader to lead a discussion about *From Broken Boy to Mended Man*. Whether you already have a group or want to start a new group, you can facilitate thoughtful discussions by following these guidelines.

PART OF AN EXISTING GROUP?

Plan to meet regularly and discuss the questions at the end of each chapter. While the book is written for men, your discussion group can include men, women, or a mixed audience. Read on for additional suggestions.

WANT TO START A NEW GROUP?

The optimum group size is four to twelve people. Assume some will have to miss a week occasionally.

Photocopy the table of contents and the questions at the end of a couple of chapters. Then give copies to the people you want to meet with. Ask them if they would like to be in a discussion group that would read the book and answer questions at the end of each chapter. This can be a group from work, church, your neighborhood, or any combination.

Ask for a four-week commitment to discuss "Part 1: Unraveling Your Childhood Wounds." If the group gels, continue with the remaining chapters.

DECIDE WHEN AND WHERE YOU WANT TO MEET

Most groups meet weekly, but many successful groups meet every other week or once a month. Due to the discussion topics, choose a location that is conducive to deeper, personal conversations, such as a home or coffee shop with outdoor seating.

DECIDE HOW LONG YOU WANT TO MEET FOR

Most groups meet for one or two hours, depending on the time of day and schedule constraints. For a one-hour meeting in the morning before work, for example, this could be a good schedule to follow:

- Ask an icebreaker question to help people open up, such as "Anyone have a particularly good or tough week?" (5 minutes)
- Discuss the questions at the end of the chapter. (45 minutes)
- Pray for each other as a group. (10 minutes)

For longer meetings, use the additional time for more in-depth discussion. Or, if you meet over breakfast or lunch, allow extra time for eating.

BEFORE YOU MEET, DISTRIBUTE COPIES OF THE BOOK

Have a copy for each member. (They can reimburse you.) Ask group members to come to the first meeting having already read the first two chapters and prepared to answer the questions at the end of chapter 2. (After that initial meeting, you may choose to cover one chapter at a time.)

CHALLENGE EVERYONE TO READ AHEAD OF THE MEETINGS

A leader once told me about a small group that got mixed results. He said, "The people who read the chapter we study before they come are growing, and those who don't read it are stagnant. The stagnant ones just can't understand why their lives are not changing."

BE PUNCTUAL

Starting and ending on time builds trust.

GUIDE THE DISCUSSION

The key to a successful discussion group is ensuring that each member gets "airtime." As you ask the reflection and discussion questions in order, encourage each person to share their thoughts, experiences, and ideas each week.

Don't talk more than 25 percent of the time. If there is silence when you ask a question, don't try to fill the space.

If you have an especially quiet group member, take initiative and address him by name—for example, "John, how would you answer question 3?" But sense his pace. If he isn't ready to talk, don't force him.

If, on the other hand, a group member consistently dominates the conversation, privately ask him to help you draw out the shy members of the group.

If a group member throws out an off-topic question that distracts from the conversation, suggest that you talk about that issue at a separate time.

And if someone asks you a question beyond your scope, simply say so and move on. You don't need to be a teacher or a counselor; your role is simply to guide discussion.

CARE

Value is what sustains a group. Every time someone shows up, he has decided not to do something else. So, what do men find valuable?

Men will come if they sense you really care about them. Life can be brutal, especially when trying to manage unhealed wounds. We all need to be encouraged.

Call or text each group member weekly—on the day before your meeting to remind them, but also to check in and see how they are doing. Caring is the make-or-break point.

NOTES

EPIGRAPH

1. This definition is adapted from Dictionary.com, s.v. "broken (*adj.*)," "mended (*v.*)," accessed May 16, 2023, https://www.dictionary.com/ browse/broken, https://www.dictionary.com/browse/mended.

CHAPTER 1: THE FRATERNAL ORDER OF BROKEN BOYS

1. Terrence Real, *I Don't Want to Talk about It: Overcoming the Secret Legacy of Male Depression* (New York: Fireside, 1998), 146.
2. Terence T. Gorski, *Getting Love Right: Learning the Choices of Healthy Intimacy* (New York: Touchstone, 2012), 29.

CHAPTER 3: HOW OUR PARENTS WOUNDED US

1. Arthur C. Brooks, *From Strength to Strength* (New York: Portfolio, 2022), 49.

CHAPTER 4: UNDERSTANDING YOUR WOUNDS—PART 1

1. Gabriel A. Orenstein and Lindsay Lewis, "Eriksons Stages of Psychosocial Development," StatPearls, updated November 7, 2022, https://www.ncbi .nlm.nih.gov/books/NBK556096/.
2. Rhona Lewis, "Erikson's 8 Stages of Psychosocial Development, Explained for Parents," Healthline, April 28, 2020, https://www.healthline .com/health/parenting/erikson-stages.
3. James Garbarino, *Lost Boys: Why Our Sons Turn Violent and How We Can Save Them* (New York: The Free Press, 1999), 81.

CHAPTER 5: UNDERSTANDING YOUR WOUNDS—PART 2

1. Patrick Morley, *Man Alive: Transforming Your Seven Primal Needs into a Powerful Spiritual Life* (Colorado Springs: Multnomah, 2012).

2. James Garbarino, *Lost Boys: Why Our Sons Turn Violent and How We Can Save Them* (New York: The Free Press, 1999), 34–35.

CHAPTER 8: HOW TO GRIEVE WHAT SHOULD HAVE BEEN
1. *Collins Dictionary*, s.v. "grief (*n.*)," accessed April 21, 2023, https://www.collinsdictionary.com/us/dictionary/english/grief.

CHAPTER 9: HOW TO FIND REST FOR YOUR SOUL
1. *Alcoholics Anonymous: The Story of How Many Thousands of Men and Women Have Recovered from Alcoholism*, 4th ed. (New York: Alcoholics Anonymous World Services, 2001), 59–60.
2. *Alcoholics Anonymous*, 58–59.

CHAPTER 11: RETHINKING YOUR PARENTS' STORIES
1. Laurence Geller (speech, International Churchill Society, opening of exhibit "Churchill's Shakespeare," Folger Library, Washington, DC, October 21, 2018), https://winstonchurchill.org/resources/in-the-media/churchill-in-the-news/folger-library-churchills-shakespeare/.
2. Sally Kohn and Erick Erickson, "Relationship across Rupture," October 11, 2018, in *On Being* with Krista Tippett, podcast, MP3 audio, 12:15, https://onbeing.org/programs/sally-kohn-and-erick-erickson-relationship-across-rupture-oct18/.

CHAPTER 13: HOW TO REBUILD YOUR RELATIONSHIPS (OR SET BOUNDARIES)—PART 2
1. Joseph Grenny et al., *Crucial Conversations: Tools for Talking When Stakes Are High*, 3rd ed. (New York: McGraw Hill, 2022), 3.

CHAPTER 14: THE JOY OF WALKING WITH A LIMP
1. See Luke 6:23; 1 Peter 1:6-7; and Romans 5:3-5, respectively.

CHAPTER 15: OWNING THE WAYS YOU'VE WEAPONIZED YOUR WOUNDS
1. Charles Finney, *Lectures on Revivals of Religion* (Oberlin, OH: E. J. Goodrich, 1868), 1:194.
2. *Alcoholics Anonymous: The Story of How Many Thousands of Men and Women Have Recovered from Alcoholism*, 4th ed. (New York: Alcoholics Anonymous World Services, 2001), 59–60.
3. A summarized version is included in my book *Man Alive*.

NOTES

CHAPTER 16: CHANGING THE TRAJECTORY OF YOUR MARRIAGE

1. Lane Cooper, *Louis Agassiz as a Teacher: Illustrative Extracts on His Method of Instruction*, (Ithaca, NY: Cornstock Publishing Company, an imprint of Cornell University Press, 1945), 43.

CHAPTER 17: PARENTING YOUR OWN CHILDREN

1. This chart is adapted from Patrick Morley and David Delk, *The Dad in the Mirror: How to See Your Heart for God Reflected in Your Children* (Grand Rapids, MI: Zondervan, 2003), 31. It is based in part on the work of Dr. Rod Cooper.
2. Saul McLeod, "Maslow's Hierarchy of Needs," Simply Psychology, updated March 21, 2023, https://www.simplypsychology.org/maslow.html.

CHAPTER 18: HOW TO BE A FRIEND TO MEN WITH SIMILAR WOUNDS

1. Alcoholics Anonymous: *The Story of How Many Thousands of Men and Women Have Recovered from Alcoholism*, 4th ed. (New York: Alcoholics Anonymous World Services, 2001), 60.
2. Marc Schulz and Robert Waldinger, "An 85-Year Harvard Study Found the No. 1 Thing that Makes Us Happy in Life: It Helps Us 'Live Longer,'" CNBC Make It, February 10, 2023, https://www.cnbc.com/2023/02/10/85-year-harvard-study-found-the-secret-to-a-long-happy-and-successful-life.html.
3. Carl Gustav Jung, *Modern Man in Search of a Soul* (Eastford, CT: Martino Fine Books, 2017), 264.

ABOUT THE AUTHOR

Patrick Morley, PhD, is founder of Man in the Mirror, a global ministry impacting thousands of churches and millions of men (maninthemirror.org). After building one of Florida's one hundred largest privately held companies by the age of thirty-five, Patrick thought, *There must be more to life than this*. Motivated by his own search for meaning and purpose, he started a weekly Bible study in a bar with a handful of guys in 1986—a study that now reaches thousands of men around the world every week. You can find the study at patrickmorley.com/mimbiblestudy. He has written twenty-three books, including *The Man in the Mirror*, named one of the one hundred most influential Christian books of the twentieth century. His passion is helping men make sense of their lives. His mission is taking God's message of love to a broken generation. He and his wife live in Winter Park, Florida. You can hear more about his story and be encouraged in a variety of practical ways at patrickmorley.com.

WOULD YOU LIKE TO READ MORE FROM PATRICK MORLEY?

If you genuinely liked this book and wish to receive more encouragement in your walk with God, Patrick has written other books to help you continue healing and grow your faith. Here are some summaries that may help you pick one or more. All of these are available on his website at patrickmorley.com.

- *The Man in the Mirror* will help you examine your life by looking at 24 common problems men face, such as identity, meaning, purpose, marriage, children, friends, work, money, decision making, time management, emotions, and how to change.

- *Man Alive* is a road map to help you understand that raw, restless energy you have inside so that you can feel more fully alive. You will learn how to transform your seven primal needs into a powerful spiritual life.

- *How God Makes Men* offers ten timeless principles from some of the most well-known men in the Bible. Like us, they felt mistreated and abandoned, unqualified to lead, and their faith was tested to the breaking point. Like us, they longed to make a difference.

- *The Christian Man* is a conversation about the ten issues men who are followers of Jesus say matter most. These are the best lessons Patrick has learned about how to lead a more balanced life, how to think about work, what makes a great husband, how to be a dad who makes a difference, and more.

- *The Four Voices* will help you understand the negative voices in your head—one of the nine characteristics of broken boys. You will learn what those voices are, where they come from, and how to figure out which voice is speaking so you can take control of the conversation.

- *A Man's Guide to the Spiritual Disciplines* will help you develop 12 habits that can strengthen your walk with Christ. Through many centuries, followers of Jesus have engaged with these disciplines to help them know, love, and serve God with greater devotion.